Scottish winter climbs

Also by Hamish MacInnes

Scottish climbs
International mountain rescue handbook

Scottish winter climbs

Hamish MacInnes

Constable   London

First published in Great Britain 1982
by Constable & Company Ltd
10 Orange Street London WC2H 7EG
Copyright © 1982 Hamish MacInnes
ISBN 0 09 463620 6
Set in Baskerville 9pt by
Inforum Ltd, Portsmouth
Printed in Great Britain by
Ebenezer Baylis & Son Ltd
The Trinity Press, Worcester
and London

Contents

Introduction

The purpose of this book is to provide a concise guide to
Scottish winter climbs. The work encompasses the best of
winter routes which, by their diversity, ensure that no one
individual has done them all. Compiling the guide meant
drawing upon the wide experience of many climbers who
helped me with a uniform enthusiasm. This is especially true
of the Aberdeen school, with whose stamping grounds I am
regrettably less familiar than I would like to be. To all these
climbers I am indebted.

There are several additional aims of this book. It should be
informative and cater for all climbing tastes. The fact that
most of the routes are marked on the photographs eliminates
the need for lengthy descriptions; after all, winter climbs
vary from year to year and indeed even within the one
season. Some of the photographs leave much to be desired in
quality, but one must remember that they were taken in
conditions where the average photographer would be
contemplating the possible amputation of his fingers. Many
are of first or second ascents and as such this collection is
unique.

I refuse to turn the handle of the safety barrel-organ and
reiterate for the thousandth time the boy-scout laws of
preparedness and 'equippedness' for every eventuality –
even beweekment. In common language, use your loaf. If the
weather's only fit for collecting King Penguin eggs, go
somewhere else – the pub, for example. If you have only
climbed on grit before, or in your backyard quarry, don't try
soloing the Shield Direct or King Rat. Try to learn a little
about snow conditions. Avalanches aren't instigated by the
Mountain Rescue Committee of Scotland, but are natural
hazards and avoiding action can be taken; for example, keep
off dangerous slopes during or immediately after heavy
snowfall. Stick to ridges and buttresses if you are in doubt

about the snow. Remember, too, that when climbing in soft snow, where natural belays are as scarce as a sober Glaswegian on Hogmanay, a deadman gives good protection.

Dropped picks, like colour telly, are here to stay and it is assumed that the user of this guide avails himself of these aids. The gradings conform to the usual I – V system and are based on the use of this modern gear, not upon alpenstocks and instep crampons! Readers venturing on Grade V's with such ancient equipment may find these routes unduly awkward.

Both times and the names of those who did the first ascents of routes have been omitted – in the first instance, owing to the great variation in both climbing ability and the number in a given party. Any one of the routes can be done in a day, assuming a start before normal office hours. Many of the gullies described in the remote corries had early ascents; who actually climbed them is often shrouded in mystery. Rather than risk the wrath of worn-clawed tigers, I have excluded any mention of who did or did not do the climbs first.

With the exception of the Cuillin sketch, maps have been omitted. Proper maps are essential for winter navigation in these northern latitudes. Much of the region is in the path of the North Atlantic hurricanes and the relevant map and a compass are as essential as your ice axe and crampons.

Hamish MacInnes, 1981

Notes on the use of the guide

Route grades, snow and ice

The most popular numerical system of grading winter routes has been adopted, I–V. These are as follows:

Grade I.   Straightforward snow climbs of not too high an angle giving no pitches under average winter conditions. However there could still be cornice problems and they could be subject to dangerous conditions at certain times.

Grade II.   This grade can present cornice problems and high-angled snow with individual pitches of a not too serious nature. On faces and buttresses the standard could be comparable to the Very Difficult standard on rock.

Grade III.   Snow and ice climbs of a more serious nature, often giving long pitches and should be regarded as routes of high standard unless one has wide winter-climbing experience.

Grade IV.   Climbs of the highest standard, which may be too short to be graded V, yet can be highly technical with sustained difficulty.

Grade V.   Routes of the highest sustained difficulty which should only be attempted in favourable conditions. Retreat can often be difficult and belays scarce.

Abbreviations

The abbreviations used throughout the text are obvious eg:
FA = First Ascent. FTR = First Traverse. ST = Stance. P = Piton. N, S, E, W = points of the compass. R = Right. L = Left. TR = Traverse. B = Belay.

Scottish winter climbing

Over the past years a very high standard of ice climbing has evolved in Scotland. For someone not versed in this sport it is advisable to attempt the easier routes to begin with (some two standards below their normal summer rock climbing standard) rather than to get into difficulties.

Not only has the technical standard of the climb to be considered, but the condition of the snow and ice, the time factor and the weather. Bad weather can blow up very fast and a simple climb in fair weather can become a fight for survival in a blizzard. During mid-winter there is a limited daylight and not only is it essential to set off at first light but one must learn to move fast and only have essential stops. Safe, fast climbing is probably the key to successful Scottish winter mountaineering.

Snow conditions

Snow is in a constant state of change and the process of firmification should be studied (see bibliography) by all who intend to winter climb. Generally speaking, firm snow and white ice give the best climbing conditions with green ice the ideal on steep ice pitches. There are various types of ice screws suitable for belaying on ice and in softer conditions the deadman is an essential item of equipment, but whenever possible try to obtain a rock belay, either natural or with peg or chock.

Often, after a heavy fall of snow, the lower gullies come into condition first and a number of these are described. Generally speaking, the big ice gullies seldom come into condition before late January and during February and March there is often adequate green ice for climbing the steeper routes. There are many different types of snow and ice and the subject is too vast to deal with in a Guide Book. Make a point of studying these, first by reading the books mentioned, and then by observing when you are on the mountains.

Avalanches

Avalanche accidents have become such a major source of Scottish winter accidents that some guidance is necessary to avoid further possible trouble. The simple rule of not climbing in gullies or on dangerous slopes, i.e. steep, open slopes, especially convex ones, *during or immediately after a heavy snow fall*, should be strictly adhered to. Some 24 hours after a heavy fall, the snow has usually settled sufficiently to lessen the avalanche danger. The great majority of avalanche accidents occur during this danger period and if you feel that you must go out, keep to safe buttresses or ridges. Slopes of 14° and upwards can avalanche.

There are two common types of avalanches in Scotland, the wet snow and the slab avalanche. The wet snow avalanche usually starts in a gully or a slope with a harder underlayer which offers little adhesion to the fresh fall, or in the case of a heavy thaw, the water can run over this harder layer breaking what adhesion there is. The hard and soft slab avalanches are more difficult to predict, but again the 24 hours rule should be kept to. Avoid traversing potentially dangerous snow slopes.

A number of avalanches fall in the spring, usually of wet snow; and the early start advocated elsewhere in the text, especially in sunny weather, should be the rule. Cornices can fall and these should be passed before any appreciable thaw has set in. Occasionally a gully whose cornice may have fallen can have a further dangerous cornice in a subsidiary hidden gully.

Judging snow conditions can take many years' experience, but the simple rules above and a working knowledge of snow structure can help a great deal in assessing a particular climb. Make a point of studying the books listed in the bibliography.

Basic essentials for winter climbing

Check your equipment with this list before you embark on a climb.

  1 Cleated rubber-soled boots.

2 Crampons.
3 Ice axe.
4 One rope per party of two.
5 Windproof anorak/cagoule and trousers.
6 Woollen mitts and overmitts. Spare mitts.
7 Balaclava.
8 Relevant map in plastic bag.
9 Compass.
10 Torch or headlamp, with *new* battery and spare bulb.
11 Whistle.
12 Food and food for emergency use.
13 First Aid.
14 Helmet.
15 Plastic bivvy sack, heavy gauge with small ventilation holes.
16 Several pitons/dead man or ice screws, karabiners, slings and dropped pick hammers on all but the easiest routes.
17 Frameless rucksack.
18 Snow gaiters.
19 Spare pullover(s) or duvet, longjohns.
20 Protective helmet.

Do not forget to leave details of your proposed route.

An Teallach
Map: os No. 19, Gairloch and Ullapool, 1:50,000

This complex of Torridonian sandstone provides one of the
finest winter traverses on the British mainland. It should not
be treated lightly and in the event of poor visibility – a
common occurrence on this mountain – escape routes are
not obvious.

The ridge, consisting of eleven peaks (including
subsidiaries), stretches approximately north and south for
three miles. It is on the eastern aspect that winter climbing is
to be found in Coire Toll an Lochan and A'Ghlas Thuill. The
latter corrie is conspicuous as you descend the main road into
Dundonnell from Braemore, with Coire Toll an Lochan
partly hidden to the left. The ridge of An Teallach curves
round Toll an Lochan in a magnificent sweep of cliff and it
has two outrider ridges which extend about half a mile on
either side. Normal access to the ridge from Loch Toll an
Lochan is via Cadha Gobhlach col. From the north the
stalkers' path starts from quarter of a mile east of the
Dundonnell Hotel, then up the Allt a'Mhuilinn to its source.
There, go left to gain the top of Glas Mheall Mor and skirt
round the lip of Coire a'Ghlas Thuill to reach Bidean a'Ghlas
Thuill (3483ft, 1061m), the highest peak in the range. From
this point the ridge running east terminates at Glas Meall
Liath which divides the two great eastern corries. The main
ridge continues to Sgurr Fiona (3474ft, 1059m). From here a
north-west branch of the ridge goes to Sgurr Creag an Eich.
The main ridge continues to Lord Berkeley's Seat, a rocky
eminence overhanging Coire Toll an Lochan. A lower
by-pass line avoids the main difficulties of this and the
following sections, a short way down from the crest on the
west side. Beyond Lord Berkeley's Seat are the four
pinnacles of Corrag Bhuidhe which diminish in height from

north to south (from 3425ft, 1044m to 3400ft, 1036 m). The crest of this section in winter can give good sport and, as mentioned, in adverse conditions can be avoided on the western side. The 'bad step' on the southerly aspect of the Corrag Bhuidhe South Buttress can be circumvented by descending to the west of the crest in a shallow depression leading slightly rightwards. You can finish the ridge at Cadha Gobhlach by dropping to Coire Toll an Lochan, or continue to Sail Liath. From the Lochan follow the slabs down Coir'a Ghiubhsachain to reach the An Garbh Allt which flows to the main road to a bridge opposite Dundonnell House. This path which takes the true left to the An Garbh Allt gives access to both A'Ghlas Thuill and Coire Toll an Lochan.

An Teallach Coire a' Ghlas Thuill
Fourth Prong (4P) grade II/III 1000ft
Photo A/1
This is the fourth gully from L, and is probably the steepest. Izfis located just L of the South Crag. NB: The other gullies to the L of Fourth Prong have been climbed and are easier.

The Alley (C) grade II/III 1000ft
Photo A/1, A/3
This the gully on the South Crag between Major and Minor Ribs. Major Rib is on left. There is usually a through route early in season.

Minor Rib (MR) grade IV 1000ft
Photo A/1
Climb crest for 200ft to steep wall. Climb this in centre by crack and mantelshelf. Higher up pass a jutting fang of rock on R. Above is a tower; ascend this by chimney on R. The ridge now rises in easy steps to merge with gully on L (The Alley). The crest above is a steep wall with a gully on R, which is followed for the upper 300ft.

Hayfork Gully (H) grade I 1000ft
Photo A/1, A/2
This is the obvious gully between the two largest buttresses.
South Crag on L, Central Buttress on R.

Murdo's Gully (M) grade I/II 1000ft
Photo A/1, A/2
A straightforward climb when in proper winter conditions.
The line is obvious.

Checkmate Chimney (C) grade IV 700ft
Photo A/2
After climbing a 30ft step follow up a 200ft snow slope to
arrive at 100ft icefall. Take vertical channel on R side of fall
for 30ft. Here the channel angles L and ends 20ft higher in a
cluster of icicles. Bypass this on R and regain gully 20ft
higher. Now climb the enclosed part of gully to end up a
200ft snow channel.

Constabulary Couloir (CC) grade II 1200ft
Photo A/4
This takes the long shallow gully R of Corrag Bhuidh South
Buttress (top 3050 ft). Lower icefall can be avoided.

The 1978 Face Route ('78) grade III/IV 1200ft.
Photo A/4
The Triangle is a snow patch on the main face of Corrag
Bhuidhe which is located above a rock barrier. From the
terrace below this barrier access is possible at either base of
Triangle, or possibly directly via icefalls. Take the slanting R
ramp above Triangle to gain crest. Finish is just L of Lord
Berkeley's Seat. The final section of the route is the most
difficult.

Lord's Gully (Lg) grade I/II 1200ft
Photo A/4
This is the long gully running up from below the summit of
Sgurr Fiona to the bottom of upper rocks of Lord Berkeley's Seat.

The Fannichs: Sgurr nan Clach Geala, 3581ft 1091m
Map: OS No. 20, Beinn Dearg, 1:50,000

This mountain is the most popular in the Fannich range and it can be reached either from the Garve—Ullapool road or from Fannich Dam via a hydro-electric road. Firstly, from the north: leave the road at Loch Droma Dam, cross dam and follow pipeline to the Allt a'Mhadaidh. Before the coffer dam close to the end of this road there is a small bridge and here a stalking path is gained. Beyond, at a junction of two burns, the path is difficult to follow. At the end of a flat area (which is suitable as a camp site) a low hillock is visible on the east bank. This is a suitable crossing place. On the far side of this knoll the path is regained. Rising up from Loch a' Mhadaidh cross the pass between Carn na Criche and Sgurr Mor and from here the east face of Sgurr nan Clach Geala is seen. You should allow about 2½–3½ hours for the journey.

The cliffs comprise six buttresses up to 800ft high separated by five gullies. The buttresses are numbered 1–6 south to north and the gullies Alpha to Epsilon. The main cliffs are protected by lower defences in the form of a subsidiary wall of snow (the Apron) and a rocky step. The route through the latter takes the angle of Slanting Gully which gives easy access. From the south the approach to the Geala Buttresses is shorter, but can be even boggier! At Grudie Bridge on the Garve-Achnasheen road, a hydro road goes up to Fannich Dam and a motorable track on to Fannich Lodge. There is a locked gate at the start of the hydro road, the key of which can be obtained during normal office hours at the power station close by. From Fannich Lodge follow the Allt a'Choire Mhor northwards. The ground is soggy and there is no path. The walk takes about 1½ hours from the Lodge.

Alpha Gully (Not marked) grade II 800ft
The leftmost gully. Normally steep but straightforward, this gully can sometimes contain two or three small ice pitches.

Take L fork. At top of gully the crest of No. 2 Buttress must be taken. This is longer than the climb and is slightly harder.

Sunrise Buttress (A) grade IV 500ft
Photo A/5
This route takes a line directly up centre of No. 2 Buttress. Start from base of Beta Gully and go up ice bulges for three pitches. Then continue in obvious gully system. At top turn overhang on L and then go up arête to top.

Beta Gully (1) grade III 700ft
Photo A/5, A/10
A fairly straightforward route, often icy in its lower section.

Gamma Gully (2) grade IV 700ft
Photo A/5, A/7, A/8
Start on L of narrow scoop on ice for 100ft. Continue up narrow slot, 100ft. Follow up for 60ft to overhanging ice wall (30ft), crux. On each side of this are smooth rock walls, B. Now climb 40ft ice pitch, thereafter the gully is easier, follow steep snow and rock steps to large scoop above Beta Gully.

Skyscraper Buttress (S) grade V 800ft
Photo A/5, A/6, A/7, A/8, A/9, A/11, A/12
The central pillar on the crag. Start in Gamma Gully to above slot and a ledge leads onto buttress. Ascend buttress by easiest line.

Delta Gully (3) grade IV 800ft
Photo A/5
The gully is climbed direct.

Sellar's Buttress (E) grade IV 800ft
Photo A/5, A/9
This is the clean-cut buttress R of Skyscraper. Start beneath rock rib on L of Buttress and take crest to obvious shoulder followed by a shattered rib in direct line to top for the last 150ft.

Epsilon Gully (E) grade III/IV 650ft

Photo A/5, A/6

The difficulties are at the start, thereafter the gully is straightforward.

Beinn Dearg

Map: OS No. 20, Beinn Dearg, 1:50,000

Access to the Glensquaib climbs of Beinn Dearg is from the Braemore–Ullapool road close to the end of Loch Broom. A forestry road starting at the old school runs up Glensquaib for two miles to terminate at the upper march of the forest. From here a good path leads up to Bealach Coire Ghranda (4½ miles). On the right are the cliffs which stretch up to Beinn Dearg interspersed by various gullies and broken before the final rise to the summit by Cadha Amadan (Fool's Pass) which provides the easiest winter climb on this side of the mountain. A stone dyke which traverses the summit plateau passing the Fool's Pass is an excellent aid in poor visibility. A good descent line continues past the pass following the top of the Glensquaib cliffs down Diollaid a'Meall Bhric to gain the track close to the upper limit of the forest by crossing the stream. In thaw conditions (due to the stream) it may be advisable to descend Cadha Amadan to gain the main Glensquaib path, or follow the dyke north-east from the summit to Bealach Coire Ghranda.

Inverlael Gully (i) grade II 800ft

Photo A/13

This is the deep-cut gully next to Cadha Amadan. It faces directly down the glen.

Gastronomes' Gully (g) grade I 1200ft

Photo A/13

This is the gully on L of Inverlael Gully. Enter from Cadha Amadan by L TR.

Penguin Gully (p) grade III 1200ft

Photo A/13, A/14

Ascend icefall at bottom direct. Above are two further ice pitches and a through route behind chockstone. Beyond, 350ft of easier snow leads to top.

Eigerwanderer (3) grade III 1000ft

Photo A/13, A/14

Start 50ft R of Penguin Gully up minor V-shaped gully. Climb direct, then slant slightly R (pass two side branches leading L into Penguin Gully and an easy TR ledge system on R). The shallow gully continues as a steep shelf slanting R. Now gain long shallow gully in upper face. This finishes at 200ft, and 100ft further go R to broad shelf leading to small saddle on West Buttress Route. Go up to cornice.

The Ice Hose (2) grade IV 850ft

Photo A/13, A/14

There is often an icefall at this section of the face. The route goes directly up this. Finish by either Eigerwanderer or Silken Ladder.

The Silken Ladder (1) grade III 1000ft

Photo A/13, A/14

Start from a point opposite middle of Lochan some 150ft R of The Ice Hose. Angle L for 350ft towards orange marked rock close to top corner of slabby region. From here one can finish by Eigerwanderer, but the route continues via an ice trough, climbed on R for 80ft. TR R to icy slab and small basin beneath icefall. Ascend steeply on to spur R of ice and regain the trough by a higher ledge. Take the ice trough and the dividing spur to top.

Papist's Passage (a) grade III 600ft
Photo A/13
The deepest of the gullies. The crux is a large chockstone
250ft up. Climb R corner.

Fenian Gully (b) grade III/IV 500ft
Photo A/13
For the first 350ft there is high-angled climbing.

Wee Freeze Gully (W) grade IV 800ft
Photo A/13
This is the R rising gully approx. halfway between Fenian and
Emerald Gullies. It seems to disappear at mid-height when
viewed from below, but it does continue. Where it
terminates, climb directly to top.

Emerald Gully (c) grade III/IV 500ft
Photo A/13
Under heavy winter conditions the gully usually has two ice
pitches. The lower one can be over 100ft. The gully line is
obvious.

Corriemulzie: Seana Braigh
Map: OS No. 20, Beinn Dearg, 1:50,000

The easiest route into the Luchd Coire of Corriemulzie
leaves the main road at Oykell Bridge following the driveable
road for five miles to terminate at Corriemulzie Lodge.
(There are very few camp sites between Oykell Bridge and
the Lodge.)
   Though a landrover track continues to Loch a' Choire
Mhor, permission to use this for vehicles would have to be
obtained. A short distance beyond Corriemulzie Lodge there
are good camp sites by the river.
   Leave the landrover track after 5½ miles, cross the river
(before this point if it is high) and strike upwards to Luchd

Coire. This coire holds the main cliffs between An Sgurr and Seana Braigh.

Descent: A good descent line is at the back of the Inner Coire – to the left of SP in photograph A/16, slanting down rightwards from the plateau. Alternatively, via the North Ridge.

Sunday Post (sp) grade III 1000ft
Photo A/16
The left-hand of the two conspicuous gullies which flank the Central Rib of the Centre Massif of the Coire. An interesting climb of character.

Press-on Gully (po) grade I 1000ft
Photo A/16
This is the gully to R of Central Rib. There are not normally any pitches, but the cornice can sometimes present a problem.

Flowerpot Buttress (F) grade III 900ft
Photo A/16
The route goes up wide buttress between Press-On and Pomegranate Gullies. Take well defined line close to R edge. Cross large raking terrace at three-quarters height, then direct to top.

Pomegranate Gully (p) grade II 1000ft
Photo A/16, A/17
This is the long deep obvious gully between Diamond Buttress and the Central Massif. Though there are several pitches, some quite steep, there are not usually any serious difficulties.

Pineapple Gully (6) grade III 650ft
Photo A/17
Reach gully by climbing R wall of Pomegranate Gully a short way below first pitch of Pomegranate.

The Rough Diamond (RD) grade IV 900ft

Photo A/17, A/18

Climb the L side of Diamond Buttress taking small snow recess at base of Pomegranate Gully. Continue up this flank to steep chimney at top. Finish near top of Pineapple Gully.

Diamond Edge (DE) grade III/IV 800ft

Photo A/17, A/18

Start L of crest, take higher of two conspicuous R slanting ramps. Continue up obvious diedre on upper section.

Diamond Diedre (dd) grade II 800ft

Photo A/17, A/18

This takes the obvious corner line on the R of Diamond Buttress. There are usually five pitches.

Pelican Gully (pg) grade II 800ft

Photo A/16, A/17

The start for this gully and Sham Gully are the same. 300ft above fork is a short ice pitch. There may be a mixed pitch higher up. The cornice too can sometimes present difficulty. This gully holds snow better than most other gullies in the Coire.

Sham Gully (sg) grade I 600ft

Photo A/16, A/17

This gully slants off R between Summit Buttress and Far West Buttress. Start as for Pelican then angle R. There are no difficulties. It exits below the summit wall of Seana Braigh to finish just beneath the summit of the mountain

Captions to illustrations

A/1 A'Ghlas Thuill, An Teallach. *H. MacInnes*

A/2 A'Ghlas Thuill, An Teallach. C = Check-mate Chimney. *H. MacInnes*

A/3 The Alley, A'Ghlas Thuill, An Teallach. *P. Moores*

A/4 Coire Toll an Lochan, An Teallach. The lochan is hidden in the base of the shadow. *H. MacInnes*

A/5 Sgurr nan Clach Geala, The Fannichs. *P. MacDonald*

A/6 Sgurr nan Clach Geala, The Fannichs. E = Epsilon Gully, S = Skyscraper Buttress. *R. Smith*

A/7 Skyscraper Buttress starts from Gamma Gully; a ledge leads onto Buttress. Sgurr nan Clach Geala, The Fannichs. *R. Smith*

A/8 Skyscraper Buttress, Sgurr nan Clach Geala, The Fannichs. *R. Smith*

A/9 Sellar's Buttress, Sgurr nan Clach Geala, The Fannichs. Skyscraper Buttress is on left. *G. Strange*

A/10 The first pitch, Beta Gully, Sgurr nan Clach Geala. *P. MacDonald*

A/11 Gamma Gully on left with Skyscraper Buttress centre, Sgurr nan Clach Geala. *R. Archibold*

A/12 On Skyscraper Buttress, the ice groove above rock bulge. *R. Archibold*

A/13 Beinn Dearg, the Glensquaib Cliffs from above the Bealach Coire Ghranda path. Cadha Amadan (Fool's Pass) is marked CA. *H. MacInnes*

A/14 Beinn Dearg from close to the Lochan. P = Penguin Gully. 2 = The Ice Hose, normally a large icefall in winter. 3 = Eigerwanderer. *H. MacInnes*

A/15 The direct start, Penguin Gully. It is possible to avoid this pitch in a 'dogleg' to the side. *G. Strange*

A/16 Corriemulzie; Luchd Coire. Above Loch a'Choire Mhor is An Sgurr. The summit of Seana Braigh is left of Sham Gully, sg. The Inner Coire is left of sp – Sunday Post – and contains Bealach Gully, The Chute and Query Cleft. The Chute is 1000ft, Grade 1, and is the wide gully located in the SE corner of the basin. It offers a good means of descent. Bealach Gully is 300ft and runs up left from the Chute (some 500ft from the plateau) to gain the plateau at its lower point. In its lower section the overhang can be avoided and the main difficulties are concentrated in the final 200ft, usually two pitches, one in the form of an ice-bulge then steep ice to the top. Grade II-III. Query Cleft gives a 350ft climb of grade III standard and is the next gully west of the Chute, to the right of the Inner Coire. It forms a deep-cut cleft and is not always obvious from below. Initially keep L of overhangs to gain long snow shelf – this is usually the crux. Steep snow for 100ft takes one into the depths of the cleft (sometimes an arch here). Continue up cleft for 50ft, then 100ft of snow to cornice. *H. MacInnes*

A/17   The western end of Luchd Coire, Corriemulzie. The summit of Seana Braigh (3040ft) is lost in the clouds on right. p = Pomegranate Gully. Diamond Buttress is right of Pomegranate Gully, Summit Buttress is between pg and sg with Far West Buttress on right. *H. MacInnes*

A/18   Diamond Buttress, Corriemulzie. Pomegranate and Pineapple Gullies are to the left. Diamond Edge = DE. Rough Diamond = RD. *R. Smith*

A/19   Looking over towards the top of Diamond Buttress from summit plateau. Diamond Buttress marked D. *R. Smith*

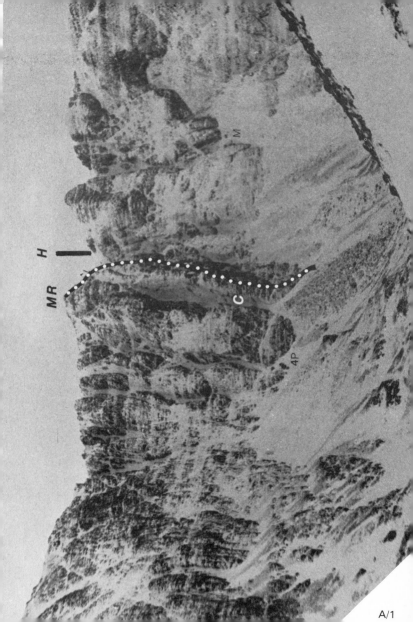

A/1

A/2

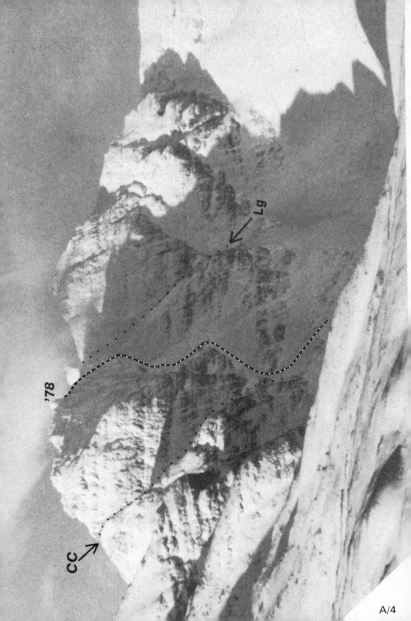

A/4

S

E

A/6

A/8

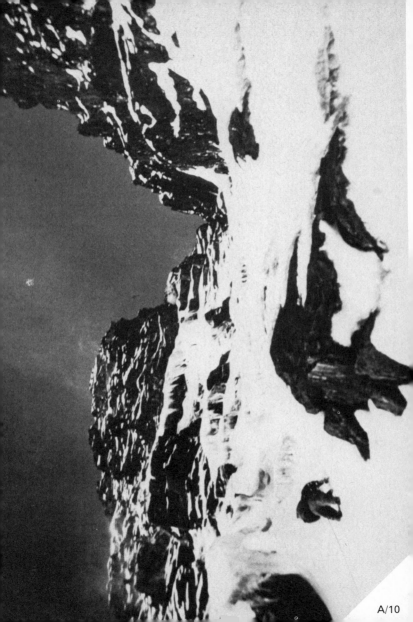

A/10

A/12

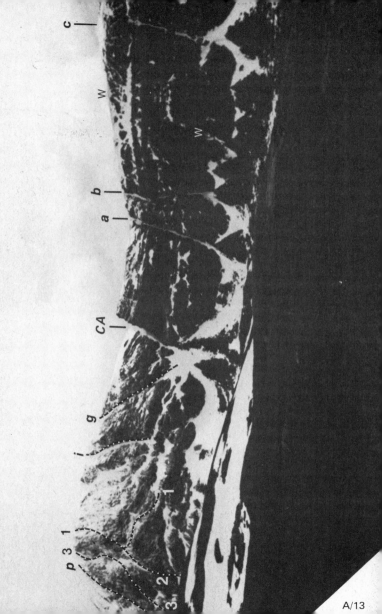

A/13

A/16

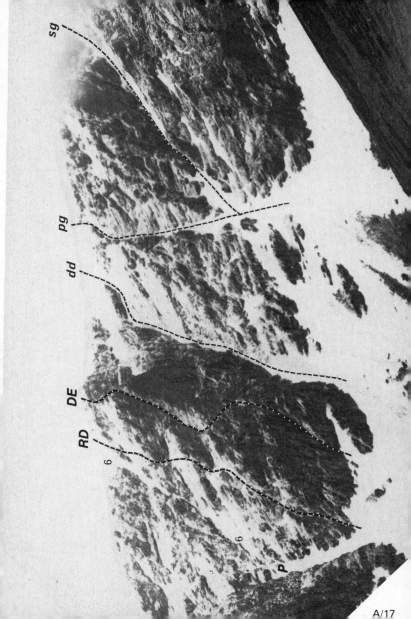

DE

RD

A/18

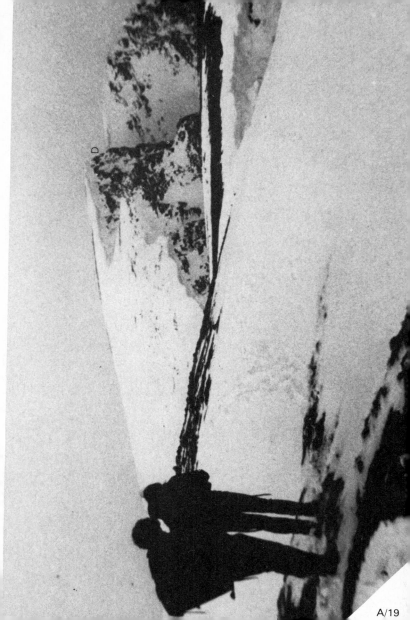

Beinn Eighe, Torridon
Map: OS The Cuillin and Torridon Hills, 1:25,000

Beinne Eighe and the Triple Buttress of Coire Mhic Fhearchair

The route to Coire Mhic Fhearchair is initially the same as that for the north-east corries of Liathach. Leave the car park on the Torridon–Kinlochewe road and take the track up Coire Dubh. Approx. a mile beyond the stepping stones slant up R on the cairned path which contours Sail Mhor to gain the entrance of the corrie in a gentle rising line. In normal conditions this takes about two hours, but this may be doubled in deep snow. An easy line to the summit ridge from here takes the Far East Gully, to the L of the main cliffs. A further easy line goes well R of the West Buttress up straightforward snow slopes to gain the crest. The crest provides a scramble up rocks, often iced, to the top.

Descent can be made to the Torridon–Kinlochewe road from the main ridge by going down the nose of Spidean Coire nan Clach (3188 ft, 971m) in a southerly direction to the car park. (Good camp sites here by the stream and ruin.) The traverse of the ridge of Beinn Eighe can be done using this route for access to the main ridge. The traverse should be considered a hard day, especially in soft snow conditions, for the complete ridge walk is seven miles with seven tops. It is relatively easy to escape to the south from various points on the ridge. The Black Carls of Beinn Eighe are encountered after Sgurr an Fhir Duibhe (heading north) and they can be tricky when iced and not easily avoided. A descent (or ascent) can be made to/from Cromasag by following the south bank of the Allt a'Chuirn, one mile from Kinlochewe, or alternatively continue from the northerly top, northwest, to intersect the stalkers' path leading down to the main road at the Anancaun Research Station one mile north-west of

Kinlochewe on the Gairloch road. The complete ridge can be done of course starting from Coire Mhic Fhearchair using the Far East Gully to reach the ridge. This entails a full day which takes in all the grandeur of Beinn Eighe.

East Buttress (EB) grade IV 1200ft
Photo B/1, B/2, B/3
Start at prominent icefall about 200ft L of East Central Gully. Gain ledge starting below and R of icefall and follow this to B at 150ft. TR R across wall and using P for tension, gain crack/corner. Climb this to B, 50ft (crux). Go up R and climb cracked pillar B on snow above, 100ft. Climb loose crack above to Broad Terrace and go up and R to B, on crest of buttress at base of quartzite tier, 150ft, TR R and climb R side of buttress for 150ft. Follow crest of buttress. S: easier alternative start along Terrace. EG: Easy Gully, grade II

Central Buttress (CB) grade V 1000ft
Photo B/1, B/4
To reach Broad Terrace climb R side of Buttress where sandstone is more broken. On lower quartzite tier climb large corner on R close to West Central Gully (WCG). TR L and then up R on easy ground to foot of final tower. Climb this on crest by line of least resistance.

P.C. Route (NR) grade III/IV 1000ft
Photo B/5
This route uses West Central Gully for access to the W side of Central Buttress where it takes a slanting line L up to the crest, gaining it close to the top.

West Buttress (WB) grade III/IV 1000ft
Photo B/1, B/6, B/7, B/8, B/9
Start close to bottom of Buttress up open scoop then a small overhang to reach snow terrace. Up R of crack, TR L across corner to slab and up this to further ledge (escape to R). Climb icy groove to sloping ledge and then on broken

ground to Broad Terrace. (Here it is possible to enter
Fuselage Gully.) Now climb to foot of final tower to gain the
80ft chimney which faces w. An overhang a short way up can
be interesting. Move L at top to gain iced slab and move up to
B below final short wall. Climb wall up steep crack to top.

Fuselage Gully (FG) grade I/II 1200ft
Photo B/1, B/10
This is the gully R of West Buttress. It starts from coire floor
and trends L between the walls of West Buttress and Far West
Buttress. The wreckage of a Lancaster bomber lies in the
gully just above Broad Terrace.

Sail Mhor 11
Gully 1 (1) grade I 800ft
Photo B/11
An easy ascent line with various possibilities.

Gully 2 (2) grade I 700ft
Photo B/11
The obvious slanting gully line starting from the scree fan
just above lochan.

Liathach and Beinn Alligin, Torridon
Map: OS Cuillin and Torridon Hills, 1:25,000

Liathach stretches east to west for five miles and comprises
seven tops, the highest being Spidean a'Choire Leith (3456ft,
1053m). It is severed from Beinn Eighe on its eastern side by
Coire Dubh and on the north-west side from Beinn Alligin
and Beinn Dearg by Coire Mhic Nobuil.
    The northern and eastern aspects of the mountain hold
the greatest interest for climbers, where three great corries
are festooned with winter lines. The winter traverse of the
ridge provides an exhilarating day but it should not be taken
lightly as the area is subjected to sudden changes of weather
and there are few escape routes, not always obvious in poor

visibility. The usual start for the ridge (east to west) is to leave the road approx. one mile east of the Glen Cottage (hostel accommodation) and gain the main ridge a short way west of the first peak, Stac Coire Dhuibh Bhig. The ridge is straightforward to the main summit Spidean a' Choire Leith. Beyond lie the Am Fasarinen Pinnacles, which if taken direct can be Grade II, but they can be turned on their southerly slopes. Continue on to Mullach an Rathain to descend slightly left to gain the Allt an Thuill Bhan. Alternatively, descend to the west of the summit (line of cairns) and go down stoneshoot to Torridon village, or continue on the wide Sgurr a'Chadail ridge to drop down to the Coire Mhic Nobuil bridge.

As well as the routes mentioned, there are other safe routes off the mountain, provided there is no avalanche danger. Some of the gullies to the south between the three eastern summits can be descended. To the east of Spidean climb down into the hanging corrie and continue the descent from here via a small gully fifty yards to the west of the obvious main gully. A cairned path follows down to the road to a point half a mile east of Glen Cottage.

Northern Pinnacles

The right flanking wall of Coire na Caime is the north ridge of Mullach an Rathain. This ridge is known as the Northern Pinnacles. It is usual to reach the gap below the first pinnacle from the north-west by traversing the lower part of the ridge from Meall Dearg on the north-west side and ascending the easy narrow gully to the gap. There are five pinnacles in all and route findings can sometimes present a problem. If in difficulty traverse out R. The climb is approx. 450 ft and is of Grade II standard. See Photo B/18.

To reach the northerly and north-eastern corries of Liathach you should leave the Torridon–Kinlochewe road at the car park close to the Coire Dubh bridge and take the good path between Liathach and Beinn Eighe. For Coire na Caime it is the same distance to go from the Coire Mhic

Nobuil bridge on the Torridon–Alligin road. (It is from this bridge, too, that the traverse of Beinn Alligin is started.) Either way into Coire na Caime takes approx. 2 hours. It is also possible to gain the Northern Pinnacles by a direct route from the entrance of Coire na Caime. This is shown as N, Photo B/16, Grade II.

Spidean a'Choire Leith
Pyramid Buttress (Ice Fall) grade IV 600ft
Photo B/12
This is the SE Buttress which is prominent from the Torridon road. The line follows the Buttress initially then takes a depression for 100ft and L into 20ft corner. Up corner, then L to ST. Climb 10ft, go L to reach rib, take rib for one pitch then slant R into large couloir directly above start. 200ft beyond, snow slope leads to top.

Stuc a'Choire Dhuibh Bhig, Liathach
Gully (1A) grade III/IV 500ft
Photo B/12
This is one of several gullies directly above the National Trust car-park in upper Glen Torridon. The route often has several ice pitches and can be grade IV in certain conditions.

Gully (2A) grade II 500ft
Photo B/12
Usually a straightforward snow climb.

Coire Dubh Beag
This is the first coire on the L as you go up the Coire Dubh path from upper Glen Torridon.

Beag Pardon (1B) grade II 650ft
Photo B/13
This gully is visible from below coire. Ascend narrow section above initial snow slope then line of least resistance to top.

Hidden Gully (2B) grade II 700ft
Photo B/13

This gully is hidden on the approach to coire. It starts on the L of the lower slopes of Access Gully. There are no particular difficulties.

Access Gully (A) grade I 800ft
Photo B/13, B/14

This is the obvious line to the col on the ridge. It gives a good means of reaching the summit ridge.

Footless Gully (3B) grade IV 700ft
Photo B/13

This takes the conspicuous icefall, the first R of Access Gully. It has been climbed direct, though various easier lines exist. The first pitch is a vertical chimney. There are five pitches.

The Hillwalk (not marked) grade II 1000ft
To the R of the coire a long slender gully trends slightly L to gain the summit ridge a short way from top. This is The Hillwalk. Sometimes a few short pitches.

North-East Corrie of Spidean
Trotters (1F) grade II 1000ft
Photo B/14

This is the prominent gully, steep and narrow, which cleaves the ridge dividing the NE corrie of Spidean and Coire Dubh Bheag.

West Gully (2F) grade III 1000ft
Photo B/14

This is the next gully R of Trotters. It is climbed direct up steep icefall.

Spidean Way (3F) grade III 840ft
Photo B/14
Take line avoiding steps on a L trend to top of face. Easier under heavy snow cover.

Way Up (4F) grade I 800ft
Photo B/14
At the back of the Corrie is an easy gully which gives access to ridge.

Poacher's Fall (5F) grade V 600ft
Photo B/14, B/15
Poacher's Fall is the large icefall which forms at the back of the corrie.
Rock Bs.

George (6F) grade III 800ft
Photo B/14
On the E of the N spur of Spidean is George. It is not seen on the approach from Coire Dubh. The upper section is the most interesting with a through route. Finish by R fork.

Coire na Caime, Liathach
This is the large corrie to the north of the main ridge. It forms a great circle almost totally enclosed by the north spur of Spidean, Mullach an Rathain, the Northern Pinnacles and Meall Dearg.

Am Fasarinen
From the entrance of the corrie six pinnacles can be seen on the main ridge ahead. The second from the left has two blunt summits with their neighbour on the right having a pointed top. These are known as the Am Fasarinen Pinnacles. The gullies in the corrie are not of a serious nature, but nevertheless give superb sport and the scenery is some of the best in Scotland.

Gully 1 (1) grade I 300ft
Photo B/17
An easy snow climb.

Gully 2 (2) grade I 300ft
Photo B/17
An easy snow climb.

Gully 3 (3) grade II 340ft
Photo B/17
The lower part of the gully is easy, but the last pitch can be
steep where there is a lack of snow, grade III. It is possible to
miss this by moving L to gain ridge.

Gully 4 (4) grade II 400ft
Photo B/17
This is the L of two gullies which form a V.

Gully 5 (5) grade I 400ft
Photo B/17
A straightforward snow climb.

Gully 6 (6) grade II 600ft
Photo B/16, B/17
There is usually an ice pitch two-thirds up gully. This can
sometimes be avoided by a through route.

Gully 7 (7) grade I 600ft
Photo B/16, B/17
An easy snow climb, access to ridge.

P.C. Buttress (PC) grade III 700ft
Photo B/16, B/17
This buttress gives a good winter line when in condition.
Climb a series of terraces. Near top take a line R of centre up
tower to gain false summit. Easier to main ridge.

Gully 8 (8) grade I/II 400ft
Photo B/16, B/17
An easy snow climb, fine rock scenery.

Upper Coire na Caime, Liathach
The following climbs are on the face of Mullach an Rathain,
to the R of Bell's Buttress. It is possible to reach this by
climbing directly from the Torridon road to the col (D) in
Photo B/18 and making a descending traverse.

Gully (1K) A grade I/II snow climb 400ft
Gullies 2T, 3T and 4T are known as the Trinity Gullies.

Left Trinity Gully (2T) grade III 300ft
Photo B/18
Between Mullach an Rathain and the Fifth Pinnacle is Left
Trinity Gully. It starts from high in the Inner Corrie of Coire
na Caime. The gully is wide and holds considerable ice
usually.

Central Trinity Gully (3T) grade II 350ft
Photo B/18
This is the obvious gully between Pinnacles 4 and 5. There
are often two ice pitches.

Right Trinity Gully (4T) grade II/III 400ft
Photo B/18
This is the hardest of the Trinity Gullies, lying between
Pinnacles 3 and 4. It usually gives a good ice climb.

Applecross: Beinn Bhan
Map: OS No. 24, Raasay and Loch Torridon, 1:50,000.

Between Loch Torridon and Loch Carron lies the
Applecross Peninsula, a rugged Torridonian sandstone area,
which, when in winter condition, provides one of the best
snow and ice playgrounds. On the southerly end of the

peninsula skirting the head of Loch Kishorn a road snakes to
the summit of the pass, Bealach na Bo (2053ft, 625m), thus
giving vehicular access (on the rare occasion) to snow and ice
climbs minutes from the car. However, to reach the main
climbing areas requires greater energy expenditure. These
are firstly Coire nan Arr which contains the shapely Cioch of
Sgurr a'Chaorachain. Though the original Nose Route of the
Cioch does not hold a great deal of ice, it does provide a long
and demanding winter route. Beyond, on the same side of
the mountain, are five buttresses and the gullies which
intersect these provide good winter routes. Access to Coire
nan Arr is from just beyond the Russel Bridge, which is a
short way up the Bealach na Bo road. Keep to the west of
Loch Coire nan Arr on a rising line if going to the Cioch
Nose, and to the valley floor initially if heading for the gullies
beyond.

The corries of Beinn Bhan can be seen to advantage from
the Kishorn–Torridon road. Though the climbs are up to
1100ft in height, owing to the lower elevation and the fact
that the area is close to the sea (and faces east) it is not every
year that they are in condition. However, during a cold
winter a good build-up of ice can be obtained and then the
corries are unique, offering wide scope. There are five
corries in all, but three give the best climbing. These are from
south to north: Coire na Feola, Coire na Poite and Coire nan
Fhamhair.

Probably the best access is from Thornapress, close to the
start of the Bealach na Bo road at the head of Loch Kishorn.
There is an old barn at this point. It takes from 1½–2 hours to
reach the corries. Two buttresses separate the three corries;
the one on the left, dividing Coire na Feola and Coire na
Poite, is known as the Cioch of Beinn Bhan. *Descent*: There
are no safe descent routes down Coire na Feola or Coire na
Poite. Coire nan Fhamhair has two easier snow slopes which
usually give access to the Coire, or the north bounding ridge
of the Coire can be taken eastwards down towards the
stalkers' path. To the south of Coire na Feola there are

various routes off the peak and it is wise to select a suitable one on the way up, for conditions do vary depending on the season. It is always possible to make the long descent south-eastwards from the most southerly peak of Beinn Bhan (2232ft, 680m) towards Thornapress.

Meall Gorm
The Blue Pillar (BP) grade IV 450ft
Photo B/21
This takes the line of the gully R of the Pillar for the first 200ft and then the buttress line is followed.

Sgurr a'Chaorachain: The Cioch Nose (C) grade IV 600ft
Photo B/22
The original route starts approx 65ft L of the true nose. For about 100ft there are a number of disjointed ledges. The top one is under overhangs. A better variation start is to the R at short crack (arrow). This is at the point where the the terrace becomes more defined. Up crack a few ft then L on to small ledge, up to spike, B. The original route is a few ft L. There are various lines up to final ledge, below overhang. The L line, up side of block, is easiest. Above, go R on ledge to obvious chimney. At top go R and take easier rocks to ledge on very nose of buttress, block B. From 10ft R of block go up steep slab slanting L; 60ft. Climb up to L of overhang above, then back R keeping to nose, small tree on ledge; 100ft. Go R to big block, up edge in three pitches, each 100ft, to top of Cioch. Continue up main ridge, past gap, on easy rock to where the ridge steepens with a gully on L. Climb steeper rock face to R of gully. Continue up over peaks and gaps on ridge. The VHF mast is a prominent landmark. Descend easily to summit of Bealach na Bo.

Sgurr a'Chaorachain: North West Buttress
Lang Tam's Gully (1) grade III 500ft
Photo B/23
This climb takes the gully to R of triangular-shaped buttress

with many small pinnacles. Climb to obvious cave. Turn this on R by icy curtain. Take R fork at top to ridge.

London-Welsh Gully (2) grade III 600ft
Photo B/23

This is the gully R of Lang Tam's. It has various branches. Usually there is ice in the lower section.

Coire nan Feola, Beinn Bhan
Suspense Buttress (S) grade II/III 500ft
Photo B/24, B/25, B/26

This is the prominent buttress on L of inner corrie. The direct start can be avoided by starting in Easy Gully.

Easy Gully (E) grade I 500ft
Photo B/26

An easy means of access to top.

C.J.W. (Y) grade V 1200ft
Photo B/24, B/25

Climb steep ice directly beneath gully to gain it above first tier. Then climb gully direct taking R fork at top.

Upper Connecting Ridge of A'Chioch (2) grade II 500ft
Photo B/25, B/29, B/30

This route can be done from either Coire nan Feola or Coire na Poite. Alternatively the lower nose and ridge can be used for access to the route (1 in photograph B/24). There are no particular problems.

Grieve's Pot (8) grade IV 600ft
Photo B/28

The route takes more or less a central line up the ridge. The start is gained via Coire na Poite.

Coire na Poite, Beinn Bhan
Alice's Buttress (A) grade III/IV 1,100ft
Photo B/29, B/30

This is the buttress L of March Hare's Gully. Start at toe of buttress on L. Up slanting R on ramp to a point overlooking gully, 120ft. Now trend diagonally L and up directly to rock band at about 750ft. TR L round a nose beneath this then up steeply to reach crest on R. Take crest to join with upper connecting ridge some 150ft short of plateau.

March Hare's Gully (3) grade IV 100ft
Photo B/29, B/30

This gully exits at the point where the A'Chioch Connecting Ridge reaches summit plateau. There are some ten ice pitches in gully, some can be avoided on L. 100ft from top a shelf leads R into R fork, take this (easiest finish).

Mad Hatter's Gully (5) grade IV/V 450ft
Photo B/29, B/30, B/31

The first 500ft of the gully is easy, with high walls. From here steep ice grooves are climbed to overhang. Turn this on the L. TR to ledge where a wall leads to another ledge, leading back diagonally R to regain gully. Follow up groove to where the gully widens and leads to easier slopes to plateau.

W.O.E.M.S. (6) grade IV/V 1400ft
Photo B/29, B/30

The central line in back of coire. Up four pitches of easy ice to gain break in first rock band. Climb this, then up R for two pitches to gain R sloping break in second rock band. Climb this, by easiest route, for eight pitches to top.

Moonshine (7) grade IV 1,400ft
Photo B/29

Climb central line of icefalls directly to great barrier wall near top. Move L 150ft and climb groove leading back R to the original line and thence on to top.

Achnashellach

Map: OS No. 25, Glen Carron, 1:50,000

The wild country to the north and west of Achnashellach
Station provides a selection of winter climbing which is often
in condition. Fuar Tholl (Cold Hole) is well named and with
its companions Sgorr Ruadh and Coire Mainreachan buttress
offers a range of fine remote winter routes.

Sgorr Ruadh (3142 ft, 997 m) and Coire Mainreachan Buttress

From Achnashellach Station on the Kyle of Lochalsh railway,
go along the railway line a few yards west of the station, then
through a gate to take the path in the forest alongside the
River Lair. The path zigzags up into the valley of the River
Lair. Beyond the slabs, which the path crosses, a cairn
(approx. 2 miles) is located at a ford. Here the path divides.
The track on the other side of the river leads up between
Fuar Tholl and Sgorr Ruadh. (Mainreachan Buttress is the
large tombstone-like rock mass to the left of Bealach Mhor.)
The River Lair path continues on past the ford, on the true
left of the river, and this can be used for access to some of the
routes on the NE face of Sgorr Ruadh.

Descent from both Mainreachan Buttress and Sgorr
Ruadh is down to Bealach Mhor, or from Mainreachan
Buttress an alternative is to continue to the summit of Fuar
Tholl and go down its SE spur towards the railway line close
to Achnashellach Station.

Fuar Tholl: The best route into the SE corrie of Fuar Tholl:
cross the railway bridge and just W of the station go through a
gate to a path (overgrown) which climbs as far as old
foundations. Take then a direct line, crossing the deer fence,
up into the corrie. Descent from the summit of Fuar Tholl is
as indicated, down its SE spur from the summit, i.e., follow
the line of the cliff.

Fuar Folly (1) grade V 750ft
Photo B/32
This route takes a rising line from R to L on lower L-hand half
of cliff. Start below obvious corner (Boat Tundra). Trend up
to R by groove/ramp to start of snow shelf. Directly up and
move R to foot of great rock bastion. TR L round nose to
recess at bottom of corner. Up corner, P for aid (20ft), then
leave corner for large face on L. Climb face in two pitches
aiming for notch on skyline (crux section). Beyond notch
trend L for three pitches.

Deception Buttress (2) grade III 500ft
Photo B/32
Start R of large overhanging chimney and take ledges and
short pitches to easier section. This leads to steep middle
section, beyond easier climbing to top.

Access Gully (3) grade I
Photo B/32

Jehu's Gully (J) grade II 400ft
Photo B/32
This is the obvious R-hand gully in corrie. Take the L wall
where gully narrows.

Sgorr Ruadh
The Slant (1) grade I/II 1200ft
Photo B/33
An easy gully with few problems, variations possible.

Steppin (2) grade II/III 800ft
Photo B/33
The obvious cornerline rising from ramp. Up corner for two
pitches, move R and continue up over a small steep step.
Continue up easier ground to top.

Robertson's Gully (3) grade IV 600ft
Photo B/33, B/34
This gully ends at a step on Academy Ridge. From well into Coire Lair the L branch of this gully can be seen. This is Robertson's Gully. It runs straight and parallel to Academy Ridge. Ascend the gully direct through a number of chockstone-filled chimneys to gain the prominent cave. Turn this on R and gain the gully again by the upper of two TR lines.

Academy Ridge (A) grade II/III 1300ft
Photo B/33, B/34
This is the longest of the buttresses. Start at protruding nose, followed by an easier section. The buttress narrows in its upper section.

Central Couloir (C) An easy route to top. From the couloir start several routes:

Post Box Gully (not marked) grade II 600ft
Photo B/33
This is the well defined gully on L of Couloir (C). It has huge chockstone near its foot. Up beneath chock (ice pitch), through route. Continue up over chockstone, turned on R to small ice pitch.

High Gully Central Couloir (not marked) grade III 400ft
Photo B/33, B/37
Just below the opposite Brown Gully is a big two-tiered icefall, which lies below a narrow gully. Climb icefall, then gully, entering the gully by avoiding the upper step on R and taking the L chimney.

Croydon Chimney (not marked) grade III/IV 600ft
Photo B/33
On the L wall of the Central Couloir is a very prominent Y gash (High Gully). L of this is a line of a chimney/gully. Climb

this and take L-trending groove, P for aid. Two further pitches to top.

Brown Gully (4) grade III 350ft
Photo B/33
This is the narrow gully starting just R of Central Couloir. Follow gully round bend to ice pitch. Up over chock and follow where gully narrows and steepens to steep groove on R wall. Up this until possible to move back into gully. Easy to top.

Raeburn's Buttress Direct (R) grade IV 1200ft
Photo B/33
R of centre a chimney splits face. Route takes line from an embayment, just R of small tongue of rock, at bottom rocks. TR up R by ledges to chimney edge. Up wall L of chimney edge. Up wall L of chimney to ledge and further terrace. Up groove L to ice-choked section, passed on vertical wall to R. From narrow terrace TR R 50ft over big blocks to recess in chimney. Go R to easier ground and take crest to top.

Mainreachan Buttress
Sleuth (S) grade V 720ft
Photo B/35, B/36
Start at arrow and cairn to R of original route. Climb crack line until possible to TR R round corner to easier rock leading up L to ledge, B. Continue up to broad terrace. To R of main barrier wall is a line of weakness. Reach this from ledge going up L to arrow, up small corner to higher ledge. TR R to reach iced groove. Up groove using spike then slightly R to near edge then back L. Directly up small wall then easier ground to under another wall to B. Up R by overhanging blocks, then directly up to further ledge. Climb directly to TR R at nose of rock (flakes above). Round nose on R and up to easier ground. Further pitch at top.

Captions to illustrations

B/1 Triple Buttress, Coire Mhic Fhearchair from the loch. *H. MacInnes*

B/2 East Buttress route, Coire Mhic Fhearchair. *H. MacInnes*

B/3 On East Buttress, Coire Mhic Fhearchair. *M. Hamilton*

B/4 Central Buttress, Coire Mhic Fhearchair. *H. MacInnes*

B/5 The upper section of Central Buttress from Western Buttress. The direct winter line up this buttress is round corner. *H. MacInnes*

B/6 Western Buttress, Coire Mhic Fhearchair. *H. MacInnes*

B/7 Looking down from the chimney on the upper section of Western Buttress, Coire Mhic Fhearchair. Fuselage Gully is seen beyond climber. *H. MacInnes*

B/8 The chimney pitch, Western Buttress, Coire Mhic Fhearchair. *H. MacInnes*

B/9 The final pitch, Western Buttress, Coire Mhic Fhearchair. *H. MacInnes.*

B/10 Upper part of Fuselage Gully, Coire Mhic Fhearchair. *H. MacInnes*

B/11 Sail Mhor, Coire Mhic Fhearchair. *H. MacInnes*

B/12 Liathach from the upper Glen Torridon road. The path to Coire Dubh goes up right of right-hand peak. A possible descent route from Spidean a' Choire Leith of Liathach comes down into the corrie to the right of Ice Fall (as viewed in photograph). Leave this high corrie by a small gully 50 yard R (west) of main gully. To descend from the east top take the main ridge over the most easterly summit to where the rock changes from quartzite. Fifty feet of steeper ground takes one beneath the highest cliffs. Open steep slopes on the south of the mountain now lead to Coire Dubh path. *H. MacInnes*

B/13   Coire Dubh Beag, Liathach. The most easterly of the three great corries of Liathach as seen from the Coire Dubh path. *H. MacInnes*

B/14   North-East Corrie of Spidean. This is the second corrie on the left of the Coire Dubh path when coming from Glen Torridon. *H. MacInnes*

B/15   Poacher's Fall, North-East Corrie of Spidean. *P. Nunn*

B/16   Coire na Caime, Liathach. This is the huge corrie to the north of the main ridge. The start of the Northern Pinnacles is on the right. The route, N, is a direct start, but the normal approach is from the Coire Mhic Nobuil path to gain a col immediately below the first pinnacle from the north-west (see details after Liathach introduction). B = Bell's Buttress. *Hamish MacInnes*

B/17   Coire na Caime from the entrance to the corrie. The higher part of Coire na Caime is to the right. *H. MacInnes*

B/18   Mullach an Rathain and the Northern Pinnacles. The Trinity gullies are 2T, 3T and 4T. D indicates the start of a possible descent/traverse line to gain these gullies from the main ridge. *H. MacInnes*

B/19   On the ridge of Liathach. *J. Cleare*

B/20   Looking across Loch Torridon to Beinn Alligin. The traverse of the summits doesn't present any great difficulty for the experienced winter climber. h = 'Horns of Alligin'. The route starts and finishes at the Coire Mhic Nobuil bridge on the Torridon–Alligin road. This is also the start of the alternative path to Coire na Caime and the Northern Pinnacles. *H. MacInnes*

B/21   The Blue Pillar (BP) from the Bealach na Ba road, Applecross. *H. MacInnes*

B/22   The Cioch Nose, Sgurr a'Chaorachain, Applecross. Approach to the climb is via snow ledges leading up left to right. *H. MacInnes*

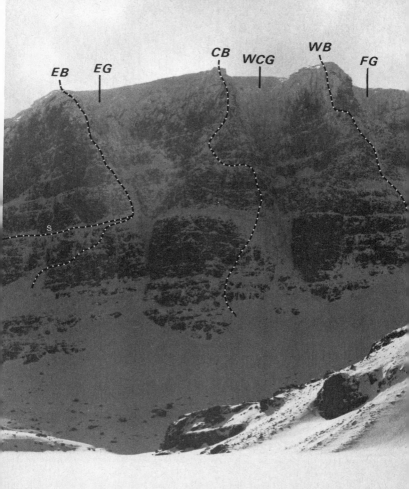

EB EG CB WCG WB FG

S

B/1

EB

B/2

B/3

CB

B/4

NR

B/5

W B

B/6

B/7

B/8

B/9

2A

1A

Ice Fall

B/12

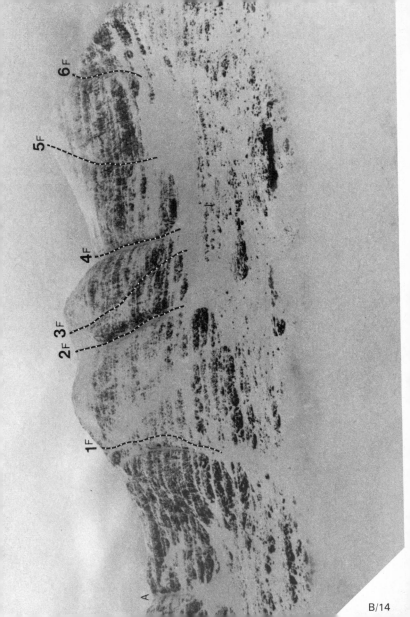

B/14

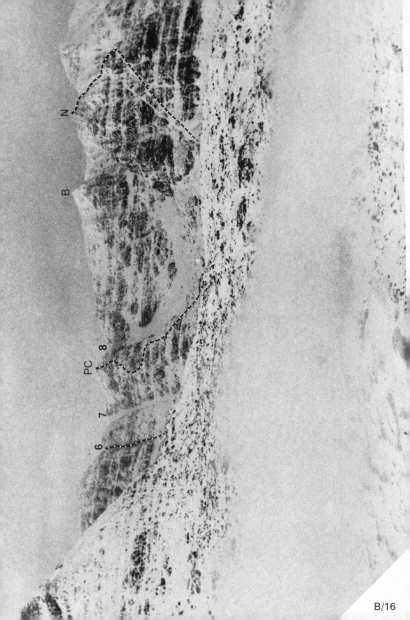

B/16

B/17

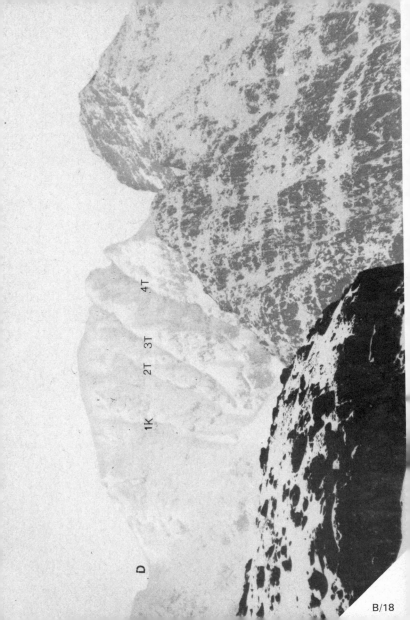

D

1K 2T 3T 4T

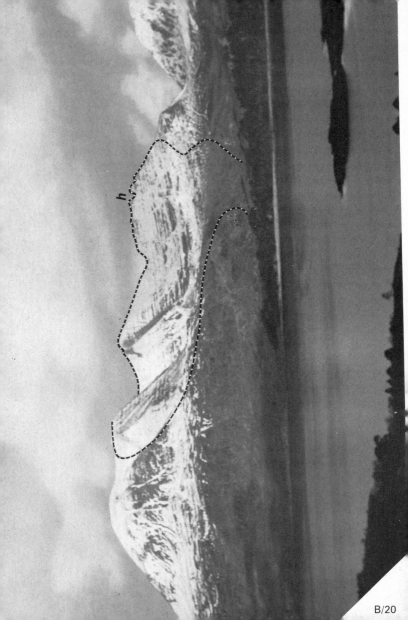

BP

B/21

C

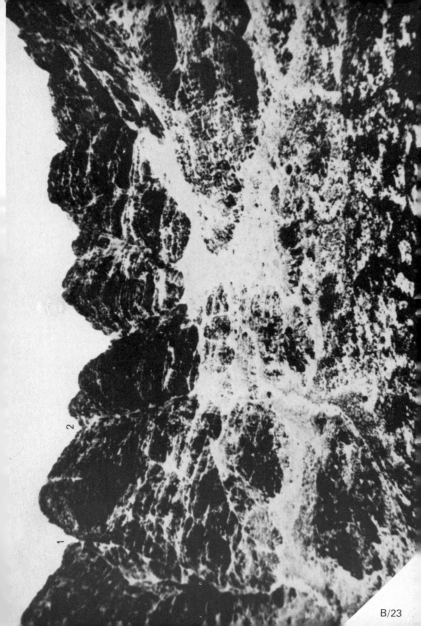

B/23

8

B/28

B/29

B/30

B/31

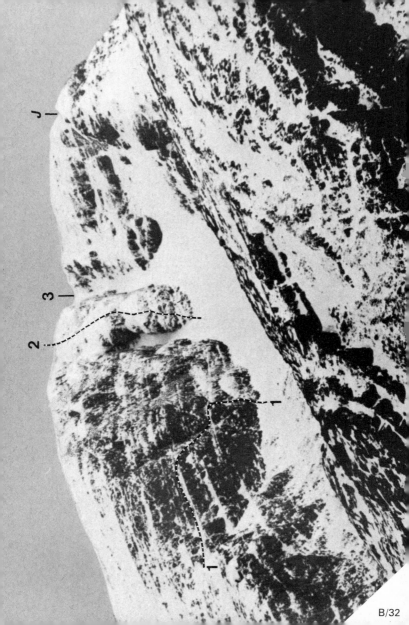

B/32

B/33

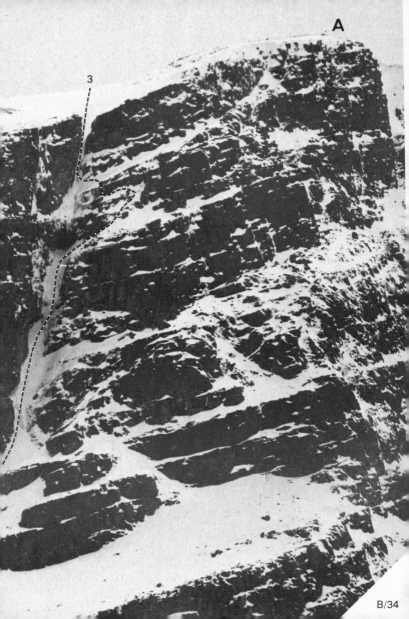

A

3

B/34

B/36

B/37

Skye: The Cuillin

Map: OS No. 32, South Skye, 1:50,000 or OS The Cuillin and Torridon Hills, 1:25,000

There has been little winter climbing in the Cuillin of Skye, due mainly to the fickle conditions. Thaws can be rapid and often one side of the ridge may have ample snow and the other very little. However, during good snow conditions the traverse of the Main Ridge provides probably the finest winter expedition in the British Isles. Nowhere is it technically hard, not more than Grade III, but due to its length much of it has to be done without the security of a rope, unless you wish to face the other penalty of more than one bivouac, or perhaps run out of conditions in the event of a thaw. It is therefore a serious undertaking and should only be attempted by those with a wide winter climbing experience and a summer knowledge of the ridge. Any party venturing on to the main traverse in winter should advise the local rescue teams as lights at a bivouac may be taken for distress signals. The ascents of individual Cuillin peaks can also give a good day out. Sgurr Alasdair, the highest peak on the island, offers several fine winter lines and even the Great Stone Shoot, as an iced-up means of approach, can give pleasant sport. There are further less ambitious climbs in winter such as the Pinnacle Ridge of Sgurr nan Gillean, many easy gullies giving access to the ridge and sections of the ridge itself.

The Main Ridge: This is done from north to south. Start either by ascending Pinnacle Ridge of Sgurr nan Gillean (allow an extra four hours for this with an average party) or ascend to Bealach a'Bhasteir from Sligachan (camp sites at Sligachan). Equipment can be left here whilst Sgurr nan Gillean is ascended (and descended) by its West Ridge. The

Gendarme is turned on the N side. At the W side of the Basteir Tooth a 150ft abseil takes one down Naismith's Route, but care should be exercised here to ensure that the correct line has been selected for the abseil. The usual place to bivouac on the first night is on the summit of Sgurr na Banachdich. On the first winter traverse the outlying summits of Bidean Druim nan Ramh and Sgurr Alasdair were included. The SE arête of the Inaccessible Pinnacle is sometimes ascended in winter instead of the steeper NW arête. The descent of Sgurr Mhic Coinnich can be done by abseil down King's Chimney. The Thearlaich Dubh Gap is the last serious obstacle on the traverse and thereafter the ridge on to Gars-bheinn doesn't present any difficulty. Descent can be made down to the Glen Brittle–Coruisk path.

Pinnacle Ridge (a) grade III 650ft approx.
Photo C/1
This is a fine winter route and a good way to gain the summit of Sgurr nan Gillean. Descent can be either by the West Ridge (turning the Gendarme on the right upon descent) or by the summer tourist route, which leads off on the SE ridge to gain the corrie leading back to Sligachan.

The best way to start the climb is to leave Altdearg Cottage, on the Carbost side of Sligachan, and cross the stepping stones to take the path to close to base of Pinnacle Ridge. Start at *a* on Photo C/1. There are four pinnacles, the fourth known as Knight's Peak. Use the snow gully between 1st and 2nd pinnacles. From 2nd to 3rd there should be no difficulty. Abseil down 3rd pinnacle on W. There are a variety of lines up Knight's Peak. This also applies to the final slope up to summit of Sgurr nan Gillean. K=Knight's Peak.

Straightforward Climb (g) grade II 250ft
Photo C/1
Follow gully line, then from col various possibilities to top.

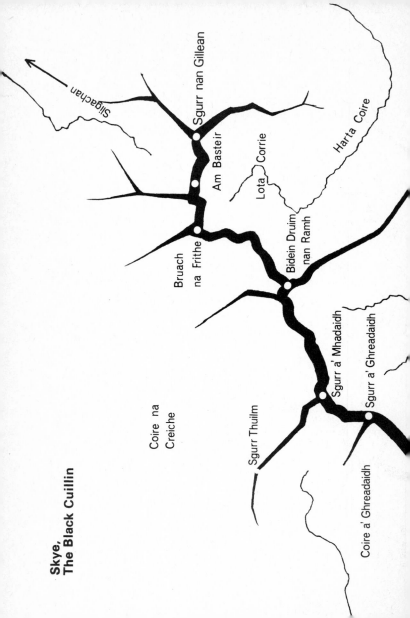

**Skye,
The Black Cuillin**

Sgurr nan Gillean

Sligachan

Am Basteir

Harta Coire

Lota Corrie

Bidein Druim nan Ramh

Bruach na Frithe

Coire na Creiche

Sgurr a' Mhadaidh

Sgurr a' Ghreadaidh

Sgurr Thuilm

Coire a' Ghreadaidh

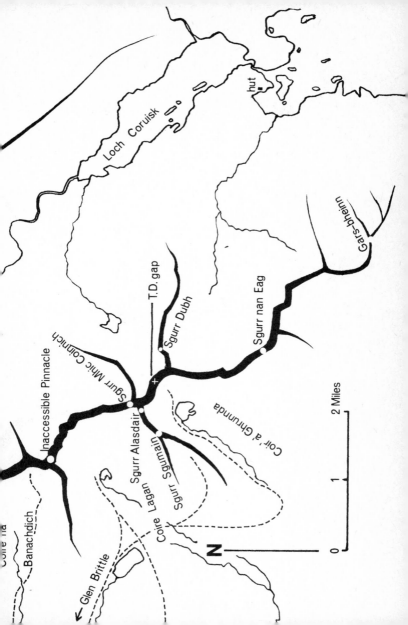

The Main Ridge

The following details will be useful to anyone traversing the Ridge.

Sgurr nan Gillean 3167ft

Pinnacle Ridge runs NNE from the summit. Also from the summit another ridge runs SSE separating Glen Sligachan on the E from Lota Coire. This ridge finishes on Sgurr na h-Uamha 2416ft. Between these two peaks is Sgurr Beag 2511ft. The tourist route from Sligachan (which keeps E of Pinnacle Ridge) joins this SSE ridge between the summit and Sgurr Beag. For the main traverse the West ridge should be taken from the summit and the Gendarme turned on the R. The cliff just past this can be descended on the N by a 40ft chimney.

Bealach a'Bhasteir 2733ft

Easy pass. L Lota Coire, R Coire a'Bhasteir.

Am Basteir 2069ft

Basteir Tooth 3005ft

Situated just W of Am Basteir. 50yds W of the Tooth a branch ridge goes N ¼m ending at Sgurr a'Bhasteir 2951ft.

Bealach nan Lice 2940ft

An easy pass. L Lota Coire, R Fionn Choire.

Sgurr a'Fionn Choire 3068ft

This is a small peak just S of the Bealach.

Bruach na Frithe 3143ft

L Lota Coire, R Coir' a'Tairneilear. Sron an Tobar nan Uaislean 1682ft is on a NW branch ridge from summit. The Main Ridge now runs S.

Sgurr na Bhairnich 2826ft

L Lota Coire, R Tairneilear. Cleft 2507ft. This is a deep cut cleft and is the lowest point on the whole ridge. Descent into Coir' a' Tairneilear down stone shoot. On the E side it is possible to get down to Lota Coire via a small rock wall just above the point where the gully descends steeply down the lower cliffs.

An Caisteal 2724ft

Bealach 2494ft

Easy pass.

North Peak, Bidein Druim nan Ramh 2794ft

Bruach na Frithe ¾m

Gap 2700ft

Central Peak, Bidein Druim nan Ramh 2850ft

From Central Peak the Druim nan Ramh ridge goes SE for 2½m and separates Harta Corrie from Coruisk. To get onto this ridge from the Central Peak of Bidein it is better to take a wide ledge on the W side of this peak and follow it to the top of the Druim nan Ramh. Near its termination this ridge has an eastward extension to the parallel ridge of Druim Hain and Sgurr Hain and then SW to Sgurr na Stri 1631ft overlooking Loch Scavaig. To return to Main Ridge:

Natural Bridge Gap 2710ft

There is an easy scree gully to Coir' a' Tairneilear.

West Peak, Bidein Druim nan Ramh 2779ft

From this peak a ridge runs NW for ½m. to Sgurr an Fheadain 2253ft overlooking Coire na Creiche. This ridge of Sgurr an Fheadain also divides Coir' a' Mhadaidh from Tairneilear. From the W Peak the Main Ridge runs to:

Bealach na Glaic Moire 2492ft
Án easy pass. L Glac Mhor and Coruisk, R Coir' a' Mhadaidh.

North East Peak, Sgurr a' Mhadaidh 2939ft
1m, SW from Bruach na Frithe.

Second Peak, Sgurr a' Mhadaidh 2910ft

Gap 2840ft

Third Peak 2934ft

Gap 2820ft
Easy descent to Coire an Uaigneis (L) by an easy rake. When a small pinnacle and a gap 24ft deep are passed, the Ridge turns.

South West Peak, Sgurr a' Mhadaidh 3012ft
L Coire an Uaigneis, R Coire na Dorus. The summit ridge runs S from the pinnacle mentioned above to the cairn 3012ft. It is fairly level. The top is a narrow crest and connects with another top of about equal height 30ft S. From the N end of the summit ridge a broken ridge runs WNW to Sgurr Thuilm 2885ft with a col at 2450ft.

An Dorus 2779ft
Descent (R) to Coire na Dorus easy from this gap.

Narrow Gap, Eag Dubh 2880ft

North Top, Sgurr a'Ghreadaidh 3129ft
This peak has a long narrow ridge with two summits as well as a small prominence just N of the main summit. NNW from this prominence and starting about 200ft down on the W a subsidiary ridge runs off which is called Sgurr Eadar da Choire.

Gap 3133ft

South Top Sgurr a'Ghreadaidh 3181ft
L Coireachan Ruadha, R Coire a'Ghreadaidh. From summit of S top a short ridge goes ESE dividing Coireachan Ruadha from Coire an Uaigneis.

Gap 2784ft
It is possible to descend into Coire a'Ghreadaidh without too much trouble. Not recommended when icy or avalanche-prone.

Three Teeth 2950ft

Gap 2925ft

Sgurr Thormaid 3040ft
$\frac{1}{2}$m SW of Sgurr a'Ghreadaidh. A small ridge goes down to Coire a'Ghreadaidh.

Bealach 2914ft
Rough descent to Coire a'Ghreadaidh; turn to R round small ridge. Descent to Coireachan Ruadha easy.

North Top, Sgurr na Banachdich 3166ft
L Coireachan Ruadha, R Coire na Banachdich. This is the highest peak of Banachdich and from the top the long branch ridge of Sgurr nan Gobhar runs to the W which ends at a cairn 2069ft. Also from this ridge the shorter ridge of An Diallaid 2375ft runs NW with a col 2365ft, possible descent by Coir an Eich which lies between Sgurr nan Gobhar and An Diallaid.

Gap 3010ft

Second Top, Sgurr na Banachdich 2089ft

Gap 2979ft

Third Top, Sgurr na Banachdich 3023ft

Gap 2845ft (pass)
From the s end of the Banachdich ridge 2887ft a spur, Sron
Bhuidhe, runs off ENE and divides Coireachan Ruadha into
two corries.

Bealach Coire na Banachdich 2791ft
One of the easiest passes between Glen Brittle and Loch
Coruisk.

Gap 2910ft

Sgurr Dearg 3209ft
From the summit a ridge dividing Coire Lagan from Coire
na Banachdich goes s then w and ends at Sron Dearg (cairn)
2012ft. The short spur on the NW of this ridge is Window
Tower Buttress.

Inaccessible Pinnacle 3234ft
The route up the Pinnacle, traversing in this direction, goes
up the short side and down the long, or it can be by-passed
on the R.

An Stac 3124ft
This is approx. 150 yds ESE of Sgurr Dearg.

Bealach Coire Lagan 2690ft
R Coire Lagan, L Coireachan Ruadha. Easy descent to Coire
Lagan via the An Stac screes.

Rotten Gully

This gully a short way along on the L gives access (in summer) to the Coireachan Ruadha face of Sgurr Mhic Coinnich.

Sgurr Mhic Coinnich 3111ft

One can either abseil down King's Chimney from the summit, or descend to, or TR, Collie's Ledge.

Bealach Mhic Coinnich 2928ft

Sgurr Thearlaich 3208ft

On the R is Sgurr Alasdair, usually done on the TR of the Main Ridge. Descent is made from Sgurr Thearlaich summit to Coire a'Ghrunnda side of top of Stone Shoot and up obvious ridge to Alasdair summit.

Sgurr Alasdair 3257ft Highest peak in Skye

A ridge runs SW to the Bad Step or Mauvais Pas and Sgurr Sgumain 3108ft. From Sgumain two other subsidiary ridges run W and NW into Coire Lagan. The principal ridge continues SSW from summit to Bealach Coire a'Ghrunnda 2759ft. To the R (W) is the Sgumain Stone Shoot, which passes beneath the cliffs of the Cioch of Sron na Ciche and to the L is an equally easy way leading into Coire a'Ghrunnda. The ridge now broadens out onto a flat stony area which forms the top of Sron na Ciche. The easy descent can be continued down this broad ridge to join up with the Coire a'Ghrunnda path.

To return to the main Ridge from Sgurr Alasdair re-ascend Sgurr Thearlaich. (From the N end of this peak a ridge, not very apparent to begin with, runs NE to Sgurr Coir' an Lochain 2491ft.) Main Ridge now runs SE to Thearlaich Dubh Gap.

Thearlaich Dubh Gap 2950ft

L Coir' an Lochain, R Coire a'Ghrunnda. The route goes down a chimney to the Gap 80ft approx. and continues up opposite wall 30ft (various lines). It is also possible to descend down gully from this point to Coire a' Ghrunnda by abseil. The rock on the SE of the Gap forms a pinnacle, then the ridge descends steeply.

Bealach Coir' an Lochain 2806ft
Easy descent to Coire a'Ghrunnda. If returning to Glen Brittle at this point, keep to W side. It is also possible to descend into Coir' an Lochain from the Bealach where there is an easy route to Loch Coruisk, cairn.

Sgurr Dubh na Da Bheinn 3078ft
Main Ridge runs S from summit whilst another ridge goes E to the other Dubh peaks.

Sgurr Dubh Mor 3096ft
From this a branch ridge goes N dividing Coir a'Chaoruinn and Coir' an Lochain.

Gap 2283ft
On the E of the gap is a steep ascent to Sgurr Dubh Beag 2403ft. The ridge continues E in a line of slabs 1m to Loch Coruisk.

Returning to Main Ridge:

Gap 2630ft
L An Garbh-choire, R Coire a'Ghrunnda

Caisteal a'Gharbh-choire 2719ft
This is a prominent castle-like rock at the head of An Garbhchoire.

Bealach a'Garbh-choire 2614ft
Easy pass. An easier route down into An Garbh-choire is to keep to the flank of Sgurr Dubh, thereby avoiding the great blocks of rocks.

Sgurr nan Eag 3031ft

L An Garbh-choire, R Coire nan Laogh. This peak has a fairly level summit ridge running SE (about 350yds). To the SW a wide shoulder separates Coire a'Ghrunnda from Coire nan Laogh. This is a route into Coire nan Laogh.

Bealach 2537ft

To go into An Garbh-choire bear L for a 100ft or so. To Coire nan Laogh see above.

Sgurr a'Choire Bhig 2872ft.

L Coire Beag, R Coire nan Laogh. A subsidiary ridge runs NE separating An Garbh-choire from Coire Beag.

Gap (a pass) 2740ft

It is difficult at first going down to Coire Beag; keep close below Sgurr a'Choire Bhig, then keep well R to avoid the slabs. To go into Coire nan Laogh keep to the slopes of Gars-bheinn at first.

Gars-bheinn 2935ft

A little S of the top a subsidiary ridge goes NE and separates Coire Beag from Coir a'Chruidh and ends on a crag. The Main Ridge continues SE to a point 2665ft. Just past this another ridge runs out NE into Coir a'Chruidh. The Main Ridge continues ESE with two prominent points, the last being 2200ft. One can also descend S and then W from Gars-bheinn to join up with the Loch Coruisk–Glen Brittle path.

Blaven: Clach Glas

Map: OS No. 32, South Skye, 1:50,000 or OS The Cuillin and Torridon Hills, 1:25,000

This ridge can give excellent sport when in winter condition. Though not nearly so long as the main Cuillin ridge, it does provide some fine situations in winter. The Clach Glas section especially can be tricky when iced up and as with the main ridge a knowledge of the summer route is of great advantage. The route, shown on the photo no. C/11, goes from N to S starting at the col to the N of Clach Glas. An iced-up chimney is climbed to the NW of Clach Glas and then the face climbed to gain a ledge system beneath the summit. The narrow section beyond the summit can be awkward when iced up if there is any wind. To reach the first col to the S of the summit a snow gully is descended (abseil) to reach a col from the NW. Gain the next col by traversing over the rocky outcrop and descending a rock step (a gully from the col offers an escape route into the E corrie). Continue up a rock step on the S side of the col and make your way on to Blaven North Top by taking a long traverse right to gain a gully to the right of the main rock face. A short descent down a rock step may be necessary to reach this. Climb gully to ridge and thence to the top of Blaven. Descent from summit via the wide gully leading into Fionna Choire (the corrie to the E of Blaven) or down the southerly nose of Blaven South Peak to reach the Camasunary track.

Captions to illustrations

C/1   The Pinnacle Ridge of Sgurr nan Gillean from the west. The West Ridge is on the right. K = Knight's Peak. *H. MacInnes*

C/2   The Gendarme on the West Ridge of Sgurr nan Gillean. *H. MacInnes*

C/3   Above Bealach a'Bhasteir with Am Basteir top right. *H. MacInnes*

C/4   Am Basteir and the Tooth. The descent route down the Tooth is out of sight on its right-hand wall. KC = King Cave Chimney and NC = North Chimney. *H. MacInnes*

C/5   The Bhasteir Tooth from the west. Naismiths is the approx. abseil line for the winter traverse. *H. MacInnes*

C/6 Looking back to the Tooth from near Bruach na Frithe. An escape route goes left here NW down the subsidiary ridge. *H. MacInnes*

C/7 A bivouac on the first winter traverse on Sgurr na Banachdich. *T.W. Patey*

C/8 The abseil down the west side of the Inaccessible Pinnacle. *H. MacInnes*

C/9 Preparing the abseil for the descent of King's Chimney, Sgurr Mhic Coinnich, on the first traverse. *H. MacInnes.*

C/10 Gars-bheinn and the end of the traverse. *H. MacInnes*

C/11 The Blaven/Clach Glas Ridge as seen from near the head of Loch Slapin. The route into the eastern corries of the mountain starts to the right of the house on the far shore, close to a bridge. Follow the true left of the Allt na Dunaiche. S = the start of the ridge for the winter traverse and d = one of the descent routes between the two tops of Blaven. Alternatively the left skyline ridge of the south summit of Blaven can be followed down to the Camasunary track. *H. MacInnes*

C/12 Approaching Clach Glas from the north on the winter traverse of the ridge. *C.J. Williamson*

NC

KC

C/4

NAISMITHS ROUTE

C/5

C/6

C/8

C/9

C/12

AREA D

The Cairngorms

Map: OS Tourist Map, Cairngorms, 1 in to 1 mile

This is the highest tract of country in Britain and the distances involved in reaching many of the climbs can, in winter, make them serious undertakings. The Cairngorm Plateau blizzard has to be experienced to be believed, and journeys into its hinterland in winter should be done with this knowledge in mind. The winter routes are outstanding and owing to the high position of many of the crags they can provide a long winter climbing season.

The ski development in the northern corries, though in many ways detracting from the aesthetic appeal of the area, does provide the sometimes weary climber with roads and chairlifts to help him on his way. The advent of the ski road and the Cairngorm chairlift has made snow climbs at the head of Loch Avon accessible for a day visit.

Coire an t-Sneachda: This is the first great corrie to the west of Coire Cas, divided from the latter by the Fiacaill a' Choire Chais which provides an easy descent/ascent line from/to the plateau. To the right of the great bowl of Coire an t-Sneachda is the Fiacaill Ridge, separating Coire an t-Sneachda from Coire an Lochan. This ridge terminates on the summit plateau of Cairn Lochan (3983ft, 1214m), the west top of Cairngorm. The Fiacaill Ridge steepens and narrows into an arête and gives a pleasant means of reaching the plateau, but it is not a good descent route. The best approach to Coire an t-Sneachda is to leave the car park at the head of the ski road and contour round the Fiacaill of Coire Cas on a path. By keeping to the east side of the corrie, the boulder field can be avoided. Alternatively, you can take the first stage of the chairlift to the Shieling and follow the line of the Fiacaill ski tow. At the crest of the Fiacaill of Coire Cas a descending traverse can be made into Coire an t-Sneachda.

Jacob's Ladder (1) grade I 350ft
Photo D/1
A straightforward route, steep in places but no difficulties.

Aladdin's Couloir (2) grade I 500ft
Photo D/1
This is the L bounding gully of Aladdin Buttress. Steep and straightforward. Follow the confined initial section then gully opens out to R, easy climbing to top. Cornice varies with conditions. Care necessary.

Aladdin Buttress, Original Route (3) grade IV 500ft
Photo D/1
The winter ascent on the buttress takes the line of the conspicuous fault on R flank, giving two vertical ice pitches, with slight deviations on to slabs on L.

Aladdin's Mirror (4) grade I 500ft
Photo D/1, D/3
Follow snow shelf going R from bottom rocks of Aladdin Buttress. Go back L up first open gully past big fault on R of buttress. Gully exits under steep snow under upper rocks. TR to the Seat, finish by Aladdin's Couloir.

Pygmy Ridge (5) grade I/II 250ft
Photo D/1
This is the R-hand triangular section on upper section of Aladdin Buttress (steep, sound, moderate rock). Climb up a rib, one section of which forms a broken, level arête. The route is obvious, overlooking Central Gully.

Central Gully, Left (6) grade I 300ft
A straightforward but pleasant route with no difficulties.

Central Gully (7) grade I 300ft
Photo D/1
This gully separates Aladdin from Fluted Buttress rising up

under the R side of Pygmy Ridge. Less steep than the other gullies of the Trident (no pitches). Often a good, but easily bypassed cornice.

The Runnel (8) grade II 300ft
Photo D/1
This is the central and well defined gully of the Trident going directly down to the westernmost lochan in corrie. Steep but quite straightforward to 120ft from top. Take L fork in narrow chimney, approx. 60ft to top slope. Sometimes heavily corniced. Rib to L of Runnel is narrow and easy.

Crotched Gully (9) grade I 300ft
Photo D/1
The least defined and R-most of the Trident gullies. Often has steep narrow section going R from snowfield into main gully.

Spiral Gully (10) grade III 350ft
Photo D/1
This gully is just R of Crotched Gully, going deep into columnar upper rocks beside Fingers Ridge as it spirals to R.

Fluted Buttress Direct (F) grade III 400ft
Photo D/1, D/5
This route is on prominent section of Buttress between Spiral and Broken Gullies. Start at line of chimneys on L of Buttress. Take R of two grooves into chimney and follow this for two pitches, slanting R to exit of crest of Buttress. Now follow crest to plateau (between Spiral and Broken Gullies).

Broken Gully (11) grade III 350ft
Photo D/1
In centre of Fluted Buttress a bay forms start of poorly defined and discontinuous gully, which goes up face L of Fingers Ridge and ends at small col a few ft below top of

ridge. Where lower gully steepens go out and climb up R side. Above a good B ledge there is a slab TR to pass round corner on L, then enter start of upper gully. Straightforward to top.

Finger Ridge (12) grade IV 400ft
Photo D/1
Take the snow slanting up L side of buttress, 120ft. Now go direct, then R and up corner, 140ft. Ascend further corner, to edge leading to Fingers. Bypass on L to base of short corner, 120ft. Climb corner, then move L into gully and to top, 100ft.

Red Gully (13) grade II 350ft
Photo D/1
This is a better climb than the Trident gullies. It snakes up steeply between outcrops and often contains much ice.

Western Rib (14) grade I/II 300ft
Photo D/1
An obvious toadstool pinnacle is situated at foot of rib on R of Red Gully, its top barred by steep rock. Ascend Red Gully and TR on to rib just above pinnacle. Climb rib (steep and narrow) then easy over blocks to tower climbed by cracks on L. A short ridge links the tower to plateau.

Fiacaill Buttress (f) grade III 400ft
Photo D/2
This is the prominent rib L of Fiacaill Couloir. Gain Rib by groove and continue up edge of Couloir. Where Rib steepens go slightly L onto Rib, then up steep pitches to base of tower with smooth wall. Pass by descending TR L. The chimney leads to easier terrain and top of tower. Beyond tower, cross narrow col at top of Couloir. A further pitch leads to top.

Fiacaill Couloir (1) grade II 400ft

Photo D/2, D/4

Often much ice early in season, later it can bank up and become easier.

Rampant (R) grade IV 250ft

Photo D/2, D/4

This takes the line of ramps followed by the big corner in the crest of upper Buttress, L of Bellhaven. Start at the alt. start to Bellhaven, at ledge slanting R. Reach the higher of two ramps leading L, follow this to where it steepens in corner. Up corner and follow ramp leading back R to B at its top. Go R into big corner and ascend this, exit through window onto Fiachaill Ridge.

Bellhaven (B) grade IV 250ft

Photo D/2, D/4

This takes the L-facing corner L of Invernookie and immediately above start of Fiacaill Couloir. Climb corner to reach ledge and B on smooth L wall; or, gain corner via ledge starting higher up Couloir. This leads R into corner. From B re-enter corner and follow it for two pitches to top.

Invernookie (4) grade III 400ft

Photo D/2, D/6

This route takes the prominent initial R fork of Fiacaill Couloir. Climb ice groove and bulge and follow snow ramp L over bulges towards steep groove. Climb this to cave. Finish R onto Fiacaill Ridge.

Fiacaill Ridge grade I

Photo D/2, D/4

A simple rock/ice scramble if ridge is kept to and the most direct way to summit of Cairn Lochan from Glenmore.

Coire an Lochain: This is the right-hand or westerly corrie as seen from Glenmore. To get to it you can start as for Coire an t-Sneachda by contouring round the Fiacaill of Coire Cas from the car park and follow the path to the stream draining Coire an t-Sneachda. Beyond this the path divides. Take the left-hand fork, then a broken path into Coire an Lochain. Descent from the climbs can be made to the W of the main cliffs, or along the plateau to the Fiacaill of Coire Cas.

The Vent (1) grade II/III 350ft
Photo D/7
Difficulties depend on snow build up at first chockstone (usually forms high ice pitch early in season). Easier above to cornice.

Vent Rib and Traverse (2) grade III 350ft
Photo D/4
The ridge of Buttress 2 bounding R bank of Vent is Vent Rib. Up rib 150ft to overhang. The arête above is steep and smooth. Go R across chimney below overhang and a long TR across wall on R round a broken corner leads to flake; 90ft. Up behind block to slant across slab.

The Milky Way (3) grade III 300ft
Photo D/4
Start up gully 30yds R of the Vent. Above a steep snow tongue is a vertical 100ft ice pitch, avoid by 50ft deviation to top of spur on R and 120ft up steep ground to gully (regained above ice pitch). Continue up gully, finishing in spiral trough in the upper Vent amphitheatre.

Central Crack Route (4) grade III 350ft
Photo D/7
The first two pitches may give difficulty if heavily iced. There are several variations in upper part, though easiest line is difficult to locate.

Ewen Buttress (Buttress 3) (5) grade III 350ft
Photo D/7, D/8
From base of Couloir up steep, broken rock 130ft to saddle.
Rock above is cut in centre by open gully. Up gully to a
rock/ice pitch. Climb crack on R, scramble to short (40ft) final
face (buttress joins plateau by a narrow neck).

Left Branch Y Gully (YG) grade III 350ft
Photo D/7, D/8, D/11
The standard depends on amount of ice. On first ascent
there was a 20ft ice pitch. It may offer more continuous ice
late in season.

Right Branch Y Gully (YG) grade II 350ft
Photo D/7, D/8
Straightforward, though a high angle. Needs good, hard
snow. Cornice can be large, giving difficult finish.

Savage Slit (6) grade IV 350ft
Photo D/7, D/8, D/10
Go round base of buttress on a terrace above broken rock
into recess holding the Y Gully branches. The slit can be seen
from here splitting wall of buttress. Up 30ft pitch to foot of
slit. First 20ft in crack up to and over chockstone (strenuous).
Crack now goes deep into buttress (easy for 15ft inwards).
Reach jammed chockstone by an outward TR. Then 50ft
pitch (exposed). Ascend edge of crack to another large
chockstone. Pass on outside. Crack can now be followed out
to top (80ft) or climb horizontally creased wall on R (II). Crack
finishes in gap in buttress forming pinnacle. Finish up
broken buttress.

Western Route (7) grade III/IV 400ft
Photo D/7, D/8
Climb N-facing rocks from cairn near centre. Along difficult
crack and ledge trending R to ledge; 70ft. Short pitch leads to
recess with smooth wall 20ft high (crux). Climb chimney

(V-shaped walls) for 50ft then easier climbing leads to obvious final wide chimney to L of small steep higher buttress. Bypass overhang at gully top on R.

The Couloir (C) grade I 350ft
Photo D/7, D/8
Easy 45° slope (fairly heavily corniced sometimes). Easiest winter climb in corrie.

Gaffer's Groove (G) grade IV 400ft
Photo D/8, D/9
Just L of Savage Slit fault up and L. Join ice groove above first roof by difficult TR. Climb groove direct, or move out R up another fault to move back L above. Follow up corner and gully trending L to upper snowfields.

Creag an Dubh Loch
Map: OS Tourist Map, Cairngorms, 1 in to 1 mile

The great face of Creag an Dubh Loch provides serious winter climbs. The face is demarked at each end by South-East and North-West Gullies, with the slanting gash of Central Gully near the middle of the face. The cliff, rising over Dubh Loch, is some 900ft high and ¾ mile in length. As with its neighbour Lochnagar, there is no close-by accommodation, other than perhaps a snow-choked howff. Access is from the Spittal of Glen Muick car park along the south side of Loch Muick and the Dubh Loch path is gained at the head of Loch Muick. The distance is 5 miles.

Descent from Creag an Dubh Loch is usually via Central Gully, especially if visibility is poor. The cornice can usually be by-passed on the left side of the gully. Other descents are: to the NW end of the cliff, by Muckle Wullie's Corrie, and to the SE end into a conspicuous snow basin.

South East Gully (SE) grade II 600ft

Photo D/12

If the chockstone is not built up with snow this usually gives a steep pitch. There is often a large cornice.

Bower Buttress (1) grade IV 350ft

Photo D/12, D/13

This route takes the line between Hanging Garden and Broad Terrace Wall. It starts at the L of two lines of weakness near the edge. 200ft of climbing takes one to the gallery. TR this to R and ascend big iced corner. Follow up steeply by a number of grooves slanting R to exit by steep prow on L. (NB: The ascent of Broad Terrace must be done before starting on Bower Buttress, or alternatively, the lower section of Labyrinth Route, which gives a further 300ft of grade III climbing.)

Hanging Garden Route (2) grade IV 350ft

Photo D/12, D/13

Climb steep gully which follows straight up from top L corner of slope – the Garden floor. Continue up chimney above. A zigzag line is now taken to overcome an undercut iced wall to gain a poor B on a pedestal beneath the vertical buttress. Reach the stepped fault (possibly by rope move) and follow this R-wards for 60ft. The fault now steepens; climb out R to good ST. on top of block. TR 50ft along ledge to join Labyrinth Route at an edge. Climb bulge above and up groove, 100ft. There is often a large cornice.

Left Fork (2a) grade IV

Photo D/13

Under the vertical buttress beneath the pedestal ascend groove above until a steep wall necessitates a L TR across icy exposed slab to gain easier terrain. Cornice may be turned on far L.

Labyrinth Direct (3) grade v 900ft

Photo D/12, D/13, D/15, D/16

This is a serious climb with poor belays. The original line of Labyrinth Route took the deviation L on the rear wall of Hanging Garden. In poor winters the bottom part of the couloir can be difficult. The steepest ice pitch, close to the bottom, can be by-passed on R. Usually the couloir is easier later in the season provided it banks up. Above the Garden the normal Labyrinth winter line takes an open chimney to an overhang 200ft above. This leads to an ice pitch of 100ft. Then move L into snow-filled groove. Climb this, slanting R at top to gain plateau. For the *Direct*: instead of TR L into Hanging Garden, follow straight up couloir by steep groove. A cul-de-sac is reached in 200ft. Turn this on L wall (overhanging slightly for 30ft). Continue up steep groove for 100ft, then the climbing gets easier for the 150ft to cornice. An adequate build-up is necessary for this route.

Labyrinth Edge (4) grade IV 900ft

Photo D/12, D/13, D/17

Start up the R bank of Labyrinth Groove. Continue up slanting R until a move L leads to big groove. Climb this to platform. Move up right to gain the 'Sea of Slabs'. Beyond, the Lower Tower is turned on R to gain the upstanding 'Fang on Edge'. Turn this on L. Above the Upper Tower TR ledge to gain chimney round R side. Climb out by R wall of this to reach easier ground. (NB: The Upper Tower is usually the crux and it has been climbed also on the L overlooking Labyrinth Groove.)

Mammoth (5) grade III/IV 1200ft

Photo D/12, D/13, D/18

From foot of Labyrinth Groove slant R up shallow grooves and slabs to reach a gully (Dinosaur). Ascend this by R branch and follow up R along snow shelves. Move out R onto easier terrain of Central Gully Buttress or finish up beneath the overhanging side walls of upper slabs.

139

Theseus Grooves (6) grade III/IV 800ft

Photo D/12, D/13, D/19

Follow line of grooves that higher up develop into troughs leading onto Central Gully Buttress. From here it is easier to top.

Central Gully (C) grade I 1000ft

Photo D/12

An easy gully, cornice can usually be avoided on L. On descent blocks in lower gully can inhibit glissading.

Vertigo Wall (7) grade V 400ft

Photo D/12

This route is easy located by scar of big rockfall. From a large block in gully bed a level shelf goes R onto face. Up and to R is a dark chimney: up directly, then 20ft from near end of shelf, TR R along top of slab, overlooking shelf to groove. Ascend groove which ends under 20ft vertical crack. Up crack (two recessed red rock overhangs above). Move R up onto big detached block. TR R, 10ft into recess. Up short wall on L to steep edge. This goes up slabs to base of dark chimney (icy). TR R 30ft, up a few feet, then cross back to L on slabs above overhangs. The TR finishes immediately above chimney at ST in corner (PB). Ascend slab straight above to loose flake and immediately make awkward move up steep inset corner followed by a delicate ledge TR to R. Where ledge thins, pull up to large ledge. Now easier to top. (NB: Various points of aid were used on the first ascent of this route.)

False Gully (8) grade V 600ft

Photo D/12

Climb initial slopes to first steep pitch (short), beneath steep wall on R. This ends on ledge fading out onto slabs. Move along ledge and enter steep chimney. Gain L arête with tension move. Climb arête and move L up short V-groove to gain platform (old P belay). Continue up 15ft recessed slab to easier terrain. (NB: Due to the diagonal line of this route, retreat could be difficult from the upper region.)

North West Gully (NW) grade II/III 600ft
Photo D/12, D/14

This is a better and harder route than SE Gully. Normally there are icefalls at entry and exit slabs. The first one can be bypassed. The upper pitch, usually steeper, is often climbed slanting up L.

Beinn a'Bhuird, Garbh Choire (MR 110017)
Map: OS Tourist Map, Cairngorms, 1 in to 1 mile

Though one of the most remote of the Scottish winter climbing corries, the Garbh Choire of Beinn a'Bhuird is also one of the most scenic. The 600-ft crag is bounded on each side by the two great 'bookend' buttresses of Squareface and Mitre Ridge. Due to the long walk into Garbh Choire (9 miles) it is better to climb here later in the season when days are longer and with luck the snow on the approach is consolidated.

Access: Leave the main Aberdeen–Braemar road approx. 100 yards east of Invercauld House; avoid the house by taking the upper road. Beyond Alltdourie Cottage gain Glen Sluggain through conifers. The initial part of this walk can be avoided by fording the Dee (various points) on a stretch several hundred yards downstream of Braemar Castle (this is only possible when the river is low). The west bank of the Sluggain burn should then be followed to meet up with the Glen Sluggain track. Continue past Sluggain Lodge (ruin) and camp sites in Fairy Glen below Sluggain Lodge, to upper Glen Quoich. Now take the stream between Cnap a'Chleirich and Ben Avon to the Sneck. Then slant left and by descending avoid the rock ribs, and thence into the corrie. For the best descent route from the climbs, return to the

Sneck by following the edge of the corrie, but bypass the slabby outcrop about ¼ mile to the south of the Sneck on the easterly face of Cnap a' Chleirich.

Due to its remoteness, climbing in Garbh Choire should be considered as serious.

South East Gully (SE) grade IV 600ft
Photo D/20, D/23, D/24
A long ice groove is the normal start of difficulties, followed by easier snow climbing, then a short step allows entry into the bay at mid-height. The gully now narrows and steepens. The crux is the second pitch, a steep groove. From the top of this it is approx. 120ft to the top.

East Wall Direct (Ed) grade IV 700ft
Photo D/20
A climb of sustained difficulties starting at the lowest point of the slab apron. At 100ft a delicate TR L leads to a chimney system (the summer line). Stepped ramps at mid-height lead below vertical wall to allow access to an ice couloir (East Wall Route). Crux. The overhangs crowning the top of the couloir are bypassed on the L. Finish up final tower from col.

Crucible Route (CR) grade IV 700ft
Photo D/22
On first ascent, icefall was well formed. Climb a gully to reach lower end of large snow shelf. Zigzag up ramps in vicinity of R-hand icefall.to reach lower end of snout splitting the twin icefalls. TR L across snout and ascend top L-hand icefall to basin. Finish on R.

Original Route (Md) grade IV 700ft
Photo D/20, D/21, D/23
The initial groove can be bypassed in the absence of hard snow. Climb deep chimney on R to gain shallow gully to reach shoulder on ridge. Climb wall. At foot of tower, climb splintered chimney (crux) to reach the platform. The

following pitch to col is also hard and the second tower turned on L. Finish by arête.

North West Gully (NW) grade III 400ft
Photo D/23
This climb varies a great deal with either a deposit of snow in R-angled funnel at top, or 100ft of ice. Start from corrie up arête which trends up round base of ridge.

Cumming-Crofton Route (cc) grade V 500ft
Photo D/21, D/23, D/25
Climb to obvious chimney (hanging flake at mid-height). TR R via icy groove and TR L at vertical wall onto stance. Follow up corner between the ridge and its subsidiary. Initially ascend R of crack below main ridge wall then climb crack to wide platform, 80ft. PB. Up crack on L wall then TR R and up sloping ledge a small wall. Continuing, follow gully to gain ridge between first and second towers, 80ft. Continue as for Original Route.

Commando Route (C) grade IV 450ft
Photo D/23
This takes the corner gully forming the R side of the cuneiform buttress. To gain this entails a TR from the R (P for tension). Continue up upper gully by R fork in three long sustained pitches.

Glen Clova MR 278763 (Glendoll Lodge)
Map: OS Tourist Map, Cairngorms, 1 in to 1 mile

Glen Clova has been included in this guide as it is within easy access of the Dundee–Edinburgh area and also because it often enjoys better weather than the more northern and western mountain areas.

Corrie Fee of Mayar (3043ft, 927m) is probably the grandest feature of the area, with cliffs of 700 ft. The Fee Burn waterfall is located at the head of the corrie. On the left of this looking upwards the south face extends to the Shank of Drumfollow and on the northerly aspect to Craig Rennet.

B Gully Chimney (1) grade III 450ft
Photo D/27
Ascend first 150ft direct, then the 200ft ice ramp. Now up an ice pitch on R and easy to top. Escape possible on upper slab.

B Gully Buttress (2) grade III 400ft
Photo D/27
This route is ascended directly from base of buttress.

B Gully (BG) grade II 700ft
Photo D/27
Usually a straightforward climb, but sometimes it contains some ice pitches. L branch is prominent deep chimney with chockstones. Easy escape on R.

Look C Gully (3) grade IV 700ft
Photo D/27, D/28, D/30
On the L of the Central Buttress is a steep shallow gully; this is Look C. The hard climbing is contained in the first 300ft and comprises two pitches. After the big ice pitch the upper section is easy-angled and uninteresting. However by climbing L a descent can then be made via a short gully (marked T on photo D/27) into B Gully. The ascent of B Gully Chimney can now be done.

Craig of Gowal (MR 235805)
Slipup (1) grade III/IV 600ft
Photo D/31
Climb the steep ice (crux) to gain corner R of rock nose. Ascend buttress to top.

144

Slanting Gully (SG) grade II 700ft

Photo D/31

This is the prominent gully L of the central area of cliff. A straightforward climb.

The Gowk (2) grade IV 620ft

Photo D/31, D/32

Start on the L at lowest point and ascend up ice-covered ledges. Spike B at 130ft. Climb short ice wall and slab to small overlap and TR R to ledge. Up shallow corner to black overhang. Climb this and following slab to ledge and B 120ft. TR down L to small ledge below small overlap and TR L to projecting ledge. Climb short wall and slab above, 80ft. Ascend crack in broken wall to L and then straight up slab to small overlap. TR R, go through overlap via rounded flake. Follow by short walls and slabs to B under large terminal overhangs 90ft. TR R under these and up iced corner to short crack. Move R across sloping ledges on the wall then up short slab to top, 100ft.

The Ptarmigan's Tail (3) grade III/IV 600ft

Photo D/31

To the R of The Gowk is a shallow depression; Ptarmigan's Tail starts here. Climb to snow basin in two pitches. A shallow gully now leads to big rock wall. A short TR L, followed by a 20ft ice pitch and a move R on ice, takes one to easier terrain and the cornice.

Winter Corrie of Driesh, Glen Clova.

This is the corrie on the left side of the glen, opposite Braedownie. To its right is the rounded outrider buttress, the Scorrie.

The Waterfall (W) grade II/III 200ft

Photo D/33

Climb direct, or via ice wall and corner on R.

145

Central Gully (1) grade II 400ft

Photo D/33

The obvious deep gully R of Waterfall. There is a short ice pitch where gully slants R, followed by chockstone.

Backdoor Chimney (2) grade II/III 700ft

Photo D/33

On L of main face is the wide Backdoor Gully. Where it bends R there is a deep chimney on the back wall. Up wall into chimney then to basin. Take ice ramp on L to snow slope and climb up corners and snow slope to top.

Backdoor Gully (3) grade II 700ft

Photo D/33

The obvious gully on main face which comes out at top of basin. Usually there is a small ice pitch in lower section. At top of basin go R and take first gully above.

Diagonal Gully (4) grade III 700ft

Photo D/33

There is a 100ft icefall descending from R-slanting chimney in centre of face. Climb this direct, or take easier corner on R till chimney is reached. Continue to basin. At top of basin ascend chimney with a chockstone behind a pinnacle on R. Take snow slope on L to top.

Pinnacle Gully (5) grade II 400ft

Photo D/33

The first deep gully R of Diagonal Gully. Climb it in several small pitches to basin; finish by top section of Backdoor or Diagonal gullies.

Cairn Etchachan, Shelter Stone Crag and Hell's Lum Crag

Map: OS Tourist Map, Cairngorms, 1 in to 1 mile.

These crags lie at the SW end of Loch Avon (loch alt. 2377ft, 724m). One way of getting there is to use the Cairngorm chairlift. Go towards the summit of Cairn Lochain and follow a stream down which goes between Hell's Lum and Stag Rocks (sometimes avalanche danger) to the head of Loch Avon. An alternative route is to descend to Loch Avon by Coire Raibert. For an early start (the chairlift doesn't operate from dawn) it is usually necessary to ascend the plateau via Coire Cas or the Fiacaill of Coire Cas (sometimes avalanche danger). From there the quickest route in good conditions is to head straight across the plateau to the site of the old St Valery (MR 002022) and descend Diagonal Gully (steep, not recommended for those carrying heavy rucksacks). It is also possible to approach the head of Loch Avon from Ryvon or Nethy Bothy (MR 020104) by going up the Nethy and over the Saddle to skirt the shore of Loch Avon. Though this route is longer, it should be seriously considered for retreat in adverse weather. There is a further route from Derry Lodge via Glen Derry, Coire Etchachan and over the Beinn Mheadhoin–Cairn Etchachan col. This takes about an hour from the Hutchison Hut (see Creagan a' Choire Etchachan). The Shelter Stone is located at the base of Shelter Stone Crag and it can hold six people. Sometimes in winter it is snowed up and then the Hutchison Hut in Coire Etchachan is the nearest accommodation.

Cairn Etchachan
Route Major (1) grade III/IV 850ft
Photo D/34, D/35

This route follows a central line from bottom rocks and ends at summit cairn. From snow basin to R of lowest rocks follow a rising band of snow trending L for 200ft, then TR back hard R along shelf finishing in steep corner. Up corner to snow bay (deep, tapering chimney on L). Up chimney – avoid top of this by awkward exit on to iced slab on L. An easier groove leads to steep, mixed ground below upper cliff. The line of least resistance goes up R-wards. A long TR is made across crests and scoops to R then an upward move leading to a rib. Climb rib then cross this and make short descent into main trough leading to Battlements Groove (four run-outs from top of constricted chimney). A very steep 50ft ice pitch in groove (crux). Go out L and make steep TR up L for 120ft leading to short rock-wall climbed by crack in its lower boundary. Finish up steep convex slopes to cairn.

False Scorpion (2) grade V 800ft
Photo D/35
This route initially takes a shallow gully which narrows and steepens to a crack. Here it slants L in an upward TR over slabs and crosses a rib to gain an upper fault. Follow this to top.

Siberia (3) grade IV 700ft
Photo D/35, D/39
The climb goes up the lower edge of buttress R of Scorpion fault (not described) and continues up hanging gully between fault and edge. Start where conspicuous ramps run up and L. into main depression. Go up ramps for two pitches to beneath the first steep section. TR R to ramps leading L overlooking main gully, to B in cul-de-sac, level with two big blocks on R skyline. From rib on R descend R to reach groove. This leads into hanging gully. Take this to top. NB: The top of this route is the continuation of False Scorpion, but is not used for that climb, which joins Scorpion.

Castle Gully (4) grade III 500ft
Photo D/35
Castle Gully is located high up in Castlegates Gully beyond a red cave on the wall. The bottom section of the route is open and slabby, but above it steepens and narrows in a 30ft

chimney pitch. Above is an overhanging crack of 12ft on L (crux). Now continue up rib of crest above – steep.

Castlegates Gully (CG) grade I 600ft
Photo D/34, D/35
A popular route dividing Shelter Stone Crag from Cairn Etchachan. One short, easy pitch in summer. Hard snow is often found in gully even in summer. Occasionally big cornice in winter.

Shelter Stone Crag
Castle Wall (C) grade III 700ft
Photo D/34
Climb obvious rib for 200ft starting from foot of Castlegates Gully. Interesting climbing follows to plateau, no cornice.

Breach Gully (B) grade IV 800ft
Photo D/34, D/37
This is the obvious gully between Raeburn's Buttress and Castle Wall. Climb steep blank section some 600ft above snow bay on R, thereafter the gully is regained. Above, a through route then a TR R leads into upper couloir. Continue easily to top.

Raeburn's Buttress (5) grade III/IV 900ft
Photo D/34, D/35
On L of Buttress, beneath conspicuous line of R-slanting grooves; climb grooves and move R round bulge to reach ST, PB, 150ft. TR L up ledges. TR L to bottom of line of weakness dividing buttress. Ascend this to base of steep chimney, B 150ft. Up chimney exit R to arête, follow this for 100ft to B, 150ft. Take ridge to top.

Sticil Face (6) grade V 700ft
Photo D/34, D/35, D/36
This takes the steep corner between the Central Slabs and Raeburn's Buttress. Climb to low ledge then a number of

ledges to base of corner. Normally there are three ice pitches
in this. Turn first two on L and the next direct, 2 P for aid. At
top, TR R across High Ledge. Go R from final chimney,
beneath overhang and by combined tactics 'climb' the 12ft
wall. Follow the arête to plateau.

The Citadel (7) grade V 800ft
Photo D/35, D/36, D/38
The lower part of the climb takes obvious chimney bounding
R of Central Slabs. Start up cracks giving two long pitches
leading to Low Ledge. Enter chimney proper and climb
three pitches passing the Gallery on R up to overhangs that
force move to ledge on L. Go a short way L from ledge, then
over small ledges and a 10ft R TR to diedre with crack on R
wall adjacent to the overhangs (lower crux pitch). Up diedre
to overhang. Go up on overhang using P, move R on further P
8ft above on to small hold on lip of overhang; then up slab
and R to base of fault, B ST on L, 120ft. Up wall on R, then
fault to big ST, PB. Ledges and terraces lead up easily to High
Ledge of Sticil Face. (Possible escape.) The route now goes R
onto the great nose. From top of fault (grassy in summer) TR
R into obvious corner. Follow up corner and chimney to
reach ridge, ST, PB, 100ft. Take ridge for 60ft and TR L over
nose and up to ST beside large flake abutting the large
overhanging wall, 70ft. Hand TR for 15ft (crux) to L and up
onto block (P runner) to follow up awkward crack to another
crack (overhanging) on smooth wall. Up crack to make move
into chimney to ST PB 60ft. TR up R following rim of
overhanging wall then up to ledge with loose block, 60ft.
Ascend fault to two 10ft chimneys. Climb on L to summit.

Clach Dhian Chimney (8) grade III/IV 650ft
Photo D/35, D/36
From the bottom L of Forefinger Gully climb crack on L
leading to groove followed by easier rock. Follow up two
further pitches to where chimney/gully ends under steep
wall. Exit to L and zigzag up 200ft towards vertical upper wall

of crag to reach horizontal ledge. Follow crack to lower step on skyline. Climb final wall overlooking Pinnacle gully by fan-shaped slab ladder. Continue to top.

Western Grooves (9) grade III/IV 750ft
Photo D/35
This takes the line of grooves between West Ridge Route and Clach Dhian Chimney, meeting the latter just below the slanting crack used by Clach Dhian Chimney. Start below grooves and follow these (shallow and wide) to just beneath first step in R skyline. Follow up ramp slanting L to gain the slanting crack. Finish is same as Clach Dhian Chimney.

Pinnacle Gully (PG) grade I 600ft
Photo D/34, D/35
An easy snow climb.

Hell's Lum Crag

Hell's Lum (HL) grade II/III 450ft
Photo D/40
This obvious gully often has three pitches of approx. 25ft. There is usually a big cornice. In a session of heavy snowfall the pitches can become covered. In thaw conditions beware of falling ice from the 'curtain' on L wall.

Deep-Cut Chimney (1) grade IV 500ft
Photo D/40
Climb from below or close to easy terraced fault cutting smooth, lower slabs. The chimney is obvious. There are usually three pitches in the chimney and the upper part of the route is easier.

Brimstone Grooves (2) grade IV 350ft
Photo D/40, D/41
This route is the apparent break in the upper cliff between Hellfire Corner and Deep-Cut Chimney. Take the angled

fault towards Deep-Cut Chimney and move up towards the groove. Continue up slab rib to beneath overhanging nose. Turn this on L and continue to B, 150ft. Make short R TR to easy snow, thence to top.

Salamander (3) grade IV 500ft
Photo D/40, D/42

Start from the base of the crag, climbing up snow slope to gain the broad sheet of ice that descends between Hellfire Corner (not described in the text) which is the corner on R, and Brimstone Grooves, which is on L. Ascend the ice L of the corner to gain the base of the steeper section. Make your way through this, taking the obvious tapered icy chimney, and then continue to follow the easier fault line (ice) above to the top of the crag.

Devil's Delight (4) grade IV/V 550ft
Photo D/40

Start up gully, then corner and crack to reach icy section (rock glacis, summer). Go L to a recess then from the top of a 10ft block go up vertical ice to PB at 80ft. Then go up two short walls to a triangular niche and exit this by overhanging icy crack for 15ft to Haven. Follow on for three pitches, then up cracks for 20ft and by a recess gain a ST below bulge, PB. Climb wall on L and go into crack in bulge (crux, summer) and follow on to second bulge. TR R to further crack, or surmount bulge to chimney recess behind large 30ft detached block, 90ft. It is now easier to top, 90ft.

The Wee Devil (5) grade IV 400ft
Photo D/40

This is the corner between Devil's Delight and Kiwi Slabs. Start up discontinuous gully just R of lowest rocks and climb to glacis about 100ft. Gain base of diedre. Climb it for 15ft then go L of detached flake. Continue up iced slab to reach easier upper grooves. (NB: It may be essential to have ice on this upper slab.)

Kiwi Slabs (6) grade III 450ft
Photo D/40
Take rake angling L to base of a gully, 100ft or climb directly from bottom. Now climb gully in two 80ft pitches to where it steepens.Go out on R wall by short crack followed by a ledge leading to a chimney. Cave and spike B 10ft above. Above cave step R round corner to ledge. Continue up slab and then to 50ft wall.

The Stag Rocks

Pine Tree Route (P) grade III 600ft
Photo D/43
Start at lowest rocks overlapping Amphitheatre Gully. Go up (often ice-covered) tongue of rock and continue slanting R. Before edge is gained, pass round corner on L then directly up, then bearing R up corner. Close to top a steep wall on L is used to turn large overhang. End up 20ft wall.

Amphitheatre Gully (Ag) grade IV 760ft
Photo D/43
The first ice pitch is usually climbed R to L, 100ft. Up snowfield and overhang to reach icy groove (P for aid). Climb groove, B on R, 120ft. TR L then up L to ice bulge. Go R round rock corner to reach bulge. Climb this to base of icy groove (P runner). Climb groove and B 100ft up on L. TR R beneath overhanging ice bulge, then up steep ice to finish on R, 80ft. Continue up snowfield, 120ft, then obvious corner on L to PB, 120ft. Follow up corner continuation with several bulges to end via a rock 'doorway', 120ft.

Braeriach – Cairntoul

Map: OS Tourist Map, Cairngorms, 1 in to 1 mile.

It is $7\frac{1}{2}$ miles from the Cairngorm car park to the Garbh Choire Bothy, Braeriach (MR 960985). The route goes west from the car park to join the path through Creag a Chalamain and thence to the Lairig Ghru. Continue past the Sinclair Memorial Hut to the Pools of Dee. Garbh Choire Bothy can now be reached by contouring SW. The Cairntoul and Braeriach climbs are within easy range of the Bothy. Alternatively, the Lairig Ghru path can be taken from Coylumbridge. Another start to the route can be made from the west end of Loch Morlich by taking the Forestry Commission road to Rothiemurchus Hut. A path from here leads SW to the Lairig Ghru track.

This huge complex of corries is drained by the headwaters of the Dee and forms an enormous snow-holding area, the greatest of its kind in the British Isles. These corries lie between two mighty neighbours, Cairntoul (4241ft, 1292m) and Braeriach (4285ft, 1295m). The continuous rim of these corries measures some four miles with the distance, as the eagle flies, between the two peaks of two miles. Taken in a clockwise direction from Cairntoul, the corries are: a. Coire an Lochain Uaine, b. Corrie of the Chockstone Gully, c. Garbh Choire Mor, d. Garbh Choire Dhaidh, e. Coire Bhrochain. c, d and e come within the area of the innermost great corrie of the sanctuary, An Garbh Choire.

Corrie of the Chockstone Gully
South East Couloir (SC) grade II 600ft
Photo D/44

In the SE corner of Corrie is a shallow rocky couloir. This is SE Couloir. Start approx 150ft L of The Shroud. Usually there are six ice pitches, being steepest in the middle. Reach top by steep prow, L of cornice.

The Shroud (1) grade III 500ft
Photo D/44
The obvious narrow gully L of Chockstone Gully. Climb to
steep ice in lower section, thereafter easier snow leads to top.

Chockstone Gully (C) grade III 500ft
Photo D/44, D/46
Start up gully to narrowing half way up, followed by ice
pitch. Easier section followed by chockstone (crux). 30ft ice
pitch above then steep snow to cornice. If cornice is big, a R
TR often gives an easier exit.

Bugaboo Rib 2 grade V 500ft
Photo D/44, D/45, D/46
The R bounding rib of Chockstone Gully. The difficulties are
concentrated in the first two pitches followed by interesting
snow and ice climbing leading to a final snow arête and the
plateau. NB: On the first ascent a sling was used to gain the
block. On the steep ramp of the second pitch two Ps and a nut
were used for aid. Below the overhang one P and a nut were
used for tension below the overhang.

Sasquatch (3) grade III 500ft
Photo D/44
TR onto face using ledge system going L. Take line of least
resistance to top. Cornice often large and sometimes
necessary to break through near top of Bugaboo Rib.

The Wanderer (4) grade IV 350ft
Photo D/44, D/47
Ascend gully midway between Bugaboo Rib and R end of
face. Follow up Rib on L. Continue without difficulty to
cornice.

Garbh Choire Mor

Crown Buttress (CB) grade III 450ft
Photo D/48
This is the buttress L of Great Gully. Start at bottom L of
Gully. Up slabs and ribs to big block by taking line close to
edge of Gully. Now slant L climbing up steep steps to corner.
This leads to chimney. Climb this, then easier to top.

Great Gully (GG) grade I 400ft
Photo D/48
Steepish, but no problems until cornice.

She-Devil Buttress (1) grade IV 500ft
Photo D/48
Follow iced grooves and snow arêtes on edge of Great Gully
for 200ft to R. TR over flake to enter L of twin iced corners.
200ft of steep climbing up this leads to snow prow breaching
cornice on L at top of buttress.

Vulcan (2) grade IV 300ft
Photo D/48
Follow obvious V groove, the lower section being the crux.

Bunting's Gully (BG) grade III 300ft
Photo D/48
The gully is climbed direct, take R fork to plateau.

Snowbunting (3) grade II 300ft
Photo D/48
This is the narrow channel of snow between Solo and
Bunting's Gully. Ascend channel to snowfield, then up ribs
and an ice pitch to cornice.

Egyptian Fantasy (4) grade II 300ft
Photo D/48
Take easiest line up Buttress to gain crest. It is possible to TR
into Solo Gully higher up, or continue direct.

Solo Gully (SG) grade I 300ft

Photo D/48

This is the prominent gully, L of Sphinx Ridge. It presents the easiest route to plateau. Usually very large cornice, turn it L or R.

Sphinx Ridge (5) grade III 300ft

Photo D/48

To R of Ridge the buttress flattens to form easy slabs. Keep close to Ridge. Ascend slabs up to obvious knife-edge at top of slabs, TR L round corner, then up slabs and edges to small col. There are now various lines: steep ground leads to corner and the slab beyond is climbed to gain pinnacle top. Go down to saddle, then up to top.

Pinnacle Gully (P) grade I 300ft

Photo D/48

The gully R of Sphinx Ridge, usually a big cornice.

Phoenix Buttress (not marked) grade III 500ft

This is the R of the Pinnacle buttresses. Easy to bottom of obvious corner. Ascend its R edge, or groove R. Follow up inconspicuous grooves for 150ft and slant R of steep nose. TR L round this to good ledge, 50ft. Up groove above, or take the crest of nose then up to piled blocks below steep wall. Step R then up short steep corner to large slab. Go up R into shallow groove then on to plateau.

White Nile (not marked) grade IV 400ft

This is the continuous run of steep ice between middle and R-hand buttresses of the Pinnacles trio. The route is obvious apart from slight detour at two-thirds height where an ice wall was avoided by a groove running diagonally L to an overlap, above which an iced slab permitted a TR R.

Garbh Choire Dhaidh

The Great Rift (2) grade IV 450ft
Photo D/49
This is the prominent chimney near centre of face. The route is obvious with the last ice pitch, being the hardest. Beyond this the chimney opens and it is then easier to top.

Boomerang (4) grade IV 400ft
Photo D/49
On L of open gully which divides Helicon Rib from main face there is a small arête. Boomerang starts in the groove behind this. Climb easy angled groove and steeper crack to B 70ft. Follow up iced rock for 80ft to ledge. The next pitch is easier, though harder higher at a wall with crack and small chockstone at top, ledge beyond. The last steep ice pitch is at 100ft (crux). Easier to top. NB: There are sometimes three 100ft ice pitches on this route.

Helicon Rib (5) grade III 500ft
Photo D/49
This is the obvious rib, the L wall of Chimney Pot. The bottom section takes the form of a narrow crest. A small col is reached at 300ft. Beyond it is easier to plateau.

Twilight Gully (Tg) grade II 600ft
Photo D/49
This climb is often in condition when rest of cliff is bare. No special difficulties.

Chimney Pot (6) grade II 450ft
Photo D/49
This is the deep chimney R of Helicon Rib. There is usually one good ice pitch, thereafter the chimney opens and easier climbing leads to cornice. This can present problems sometimes.

Pisa (7) grade II 500ft

Photo D/49

On the buttress R of Chimney Pot is Pisa. Start at L at easy-angled ribs. Now take the easiest line, usually close to Chimney Pot, until half way approx., then slant R to easier terrain. A ridge leads to plateau.

Coire Bhrochain, Braeriach

Pioneers Recess Route (1) grade II 700ft

Photo D/50, D/51

Start lowest point of L rocks on West Buttress and move L on steep slabs and snow to reach main fault. A series of short steep pitches leads to a widening of the chimney and steep snow leads to top. Cornice can be big.

Direct Route (2) grade IV 700ft

Photo D/50, D/51

Take a line of iced grooves just R of lowest rocks on West Buttress. These lead to a chimney often blocked with ice. Climb this and the flake above and take short steep walls and grooves slanting towards bottom of R side of large square-topped tower at top of buttress. Ascend the R side of this via steep iced chimneys.

Western Couloir (wc) grade III 650ft

Photo D/50, D/53, D/54

In the middle of West Buttress is a shallow depression. This is Western Couloir. Climb lower slabs direct, crossing Vanishing Shelf and continue up Couloir to big cornice.

The Great Couloir (3) grade II/III 600ft

Photo D/50

If the chockstone is covered this can be a straightforward snow climb. However, if the chockstone is bare the route can be hard. There is usually a large cornice.

Domed Ridge (4) grade III 600ft

Photo D/50

To R of Great Couloir is an obvious ridge. Slabs and grooves
lead to tower which is ascended by narrow chimney.
Continue over dome to wall (crux). Climb wall and then to
summit plateau.

Campion Gully (c) grade II 400ft

Photo D/50

This route runs up L from West Gully. Ascend direct to
usually large cornice.

West Gully (W) grade I 400ft

Photo D/50

The easiest route from corrie to plateau.

Brochain Slabs (5) grade III 650ft

Photo D/50

The Black Pinnacle on the L of Central Buttress is a
prominent feature. On its L is an obvious wall which runs
down to Brochain slabs forming large fault. This is to L of
lowest point of Buttress. Ascend from directly beneath fault
by iced slabs and corners to gain chimney (NW Chimney).
This runs to col behind Black Pinnacle. Ascend up and L to
prominent cave, then, still continuing L-wards trend, climb
slabs to plateau.

South Face (6) grade III 700ft

Photo D/50

This route starts just R of bottom rocks of Central Buttress.
Go directly via by slabs and grooves to conspicuous terrace
(ST). From here on the R of prominent recess take a direct
route to top.

East Gully (E) grade I 500ft

Photo D/50

No problems until cornice and this is usually avoided to R.

Thisbe (7) grade III 400ft

Photo D/50

The first gully R of East Gully is Pyramus (an easy angled snow gully). Thisbe is the narrow gully to the R of this. Climb it direct, there can be five ice pitches.

Nimus (8) grade III 500ft

Photo D/50, D/52

This is on steep buttress and forming R wall of Thisbe. There is a huge rock scar at mid-height. Gain obvious snow ramp by climbing up R. This is beneath the overhanging central area of buttress. Continue R to reach depression and then continue to large snow basin (Rock Scar). TR L and up snow rib by two pitches to plateau.

Quartzvein Edge (1) grade III 400ft

Photo D/55

The route takes L edge of Bastion past detached rock (cairn). Climb short wall and follow edge for 120ft. Continue up groove slanting L by crack, iced slabs at top. Up further slabs to lower of two shelves. TR R up to higher shelf. Up open chimney. False tower above is usually the crux. Climb this by R wall.

Bastion Wall, (Direct Variation) (2) grade IV 500ft

Photo D/55, D/57

There are no particular difficulties to the pedestal (a 7ft rock). Beyond go R to chimney (a continuation of the Direct Variation groove) and ascend this, slanting R to large ledge. Block B on R. Reach L-slanting ramp by hand-traversing block and reach further ledge in 40ft. Climb narrow groove above to exit snow.

Original Route (O) grade IV 450ft

Photo D/55

Start to R of lowest rocks on R of buttress and go up easy depression to steep wall, 150ft. Avoid wall on L then move R

161

to 7ft pedestal. Follow on to large platform to R. A few feet R climb direct for 30ft; move R across chimney onto rib and move into corner. Climb this to platform. Ascend 12ft wall behind by chimney crack to second platform with groove above. Move L to much larger V groove (directly above obvious red slab). Climb for 80ft to easier snow. Continue to plateau.

Talisman (3) grade IV 320ft
Photo D/55
This takes the R edge of Bastion on edge of Corridor. From ledge between two big rocks against wall, 20ft up Corridor. Up crack to rear of block to ledge – 40ft. Go R then up big slab to PB; 40ft. TRL 50ft to ST (crux). Go L round overhang and up crest to flake in corner. Go L to groove and climb to below overhanging corner 70ft. Corner climbed using peg and the final crest turned on L by iced groove. NB: Familiarity with the summer route is advisable.

The Corridor (C) grade III/IV 300ft
Photo D/55, D/56
A popular winter climb with usually two main ice pitches. One is over the jammed blocks leading into the cave and the other following. One of these two pitches is usually the crux. Usually there is a formidable cornice, take this on the L.

Architrave (a) grade III/IV 400ft
Photo D/55
The groove of Architrave forms a spectacular ice ribbon on the R side of Corridor. Climb groove directly to below chimney continuation. Go either direct or move L across obvious ramp to finish as for the Corridor.

Pikestaff (4) grade IV 350ft
Photo D/55
This takes the L rib, giving a mixed, sustained route on rock and ice. It is possible to escape into Central Chimney from the crest. The last pitch of 80ft is usually the crux.

Central Chimney (5) grade III 350ft

Photo D/55

The first cleft is occasionally difficult if there is little ice and can be bypassed on the Corridor or the Square Cut Gully side. 300ft of climbing in chimney, over several ice pitches, takes one to obvious R-slanting snow ramp. Continue up to cornice.

Square Cut Gully (S) grade IV 500ft

Photo D/55

The dominating feature of this gully is the large ice pillar at the big overhang. The first 250ft usually gives straightforward climbing. The first vertical ice pillar may require aid. The final slab pitch may also give problems. At the short corner, a sling and P was used.

Winter Route (6) grade III 500ft

Photo D/55

Start as for Square Cut Gully below first major ice pitch then TR onto Pioneer Buttress on R. Follow buttress rib, then a L TR. Sometimes there is a 50ft ice pitch at top.

Bodkin (7) grade IV 450ft

Photo D/55, D/59

Gain upper scoop via the terraces, 150ft. From L end go up then L to gain groove with poised slab beyond. Cross slab at lower end on rising line some 20ft above summer line (hard). Climb rib at far side to B. Go up and R TR to 40ft groove. Climb this – awkward above to large recess. Up cracked wall on R. Easy to top.

Flanking Ribs (8) grade IV 550ft

Photo D/55, D/58

Climb on ribs L of Red Chimney to gain bay below final icefall of Red Chimney. TR across chimney and ascend rib on R (crux).

Red Chimney (RC) grade IV 500ft

Photo D/55

This route is usually in condition. Start is usually up twin corners on R and the chimney reached higher up by iced slabs (lower crux). Climb chimney direct now to bottom of upper amphitheatre. Now find a route up L through ice bulges to final corner. This too can be difficult. It is also possible to finish up Flanking Ribs.

Djibangi (9) grade V 520ft

Photo D/55

This route takes the L diedre and is often well iced over. Sometimes two pitches up iced slabs allows entry into corner. Continue up corner to ST on rib (hard). Above steep snow leads to steep slab, sometimes iced (100ft crux). Easier to top.

The Dagger (10) grade IV 350ft

Photo D/55

Dagger is the R-hand corner. Go up steeply and make awkward R TR to base of diedre, 80ft. Up crack for 20ft and follow up groove. Continue to ST beneath overhang. Make awkward move round bulge and step L. Rejoin groove and follow this, or TR L at prominent ledge and ascend similar groove further L. From a good ledge under last slab a declining ledge runs down R. Go up slab via crack trending R. Then up direct L. In normal good winter conditions the final pitch will be the crux. It is possible to escape down gangway beneath this pitch, in which case the route would probably be III/IV.

Lochnagar

Map: OS Tourist Map, Cairngorms, 1 in to 1 mile

The climbs of Lochnagar (Cac Carn Beag 3786ft, 1154m) are located in its NE corrie. The cliffs, almost a mile long and up to 750ft in height, curve round the loch from which the mountain derives its name. Access is from Spittal of Glen Muick car park to the T-junction on the private road, beyond the Muick. Beside Allt na Giubhsaich Lodge a path follows a fence west through pines to a rough track. Follow it up to Muick–Gelder col and from here a path leads to the summit plateau. Beyond Foxes' Well cross the pass between Cuidhe Crom and Meikle Pap to the corrie. The distance is approx. 4½ miles.

Central Buttress (1) grade II 700ft
Photo D/60
The first and easiest of the buttresses. Climb gully slanting L. TR R above gully to gain crest and two easy gendarmes. NB: On L snow rakes run through ribs to steep slopes near plateau, giving 800ft routes.

Shallow Gully (Sg) grade IV 900ft
Photo D/61, D/63
Between Shadow Buttress A and Central Buttress there is a shallow depression. This is Shallow Gully. The difficulties are concentrated in the lower section taking the form of ice bulges and grooves where route finding is necessary. The angle eases after 200ft and steep snow takes one to the upper slopes of Central Buttress.

Original Route, Shadow Buttress A (2) grade III 1000ft
Photo D/61
Take the gully leading to Spiral Terrace to high ledge overlooking Shadow Couloir. From the top end of this ledge ascend narrow rib beside Shadow Chimney for approx. 100ft. At top of chimney go L initially, then R in short pitches to crest and small tower. The tower can present a final problem.

Giant's Head Chimney (3) grade IV 700ft
Photo D/61
This is the R of Shadow Couloir Chimneys. Start in bay at foot of Polyphemus Gully (the true dividing line between Buttresses A and B). Climb narrow gully over chockstone to below overhangs. TR R to gain wide icy trough. Climb trough to crest of Buttress A.

Giant's Head Chimney Direct (3a) grade IV 700ft
Photo D/61
At top of first pitch of Giant's Head Chimney TR L below
overhangs and go up to ST on L. Up R and climb prominent
icy groove then to upper bay to gain crest of Giant's Head
arête on R.

Polyphemus Gully (P) grade IV 600ft
Photo D/60, D/61, D/66
A very variable gully which gives a series of 6 or 7 ice pitches
or blanks out to a very high angle snow slope. In general the
gully is climbed direct with some divergence on to the side
walls when need be. The cornice, which may be large, can be
outflanked to the R.

Bell's Route, Shadow Buttress B (4) grade IV 750ft
Photo D/60, D/61, D/68, D/69
Start at conspicuous break on the DG Gully side of buttress.
The summer crux pitch is reached after 200ft of
progressively difficult climbing. From the L tooth move L
across wall to flake handrail (P for aid may be needed). Now
climb groove to B (cairn) on platform at top of steep section.
Finish up crest on snow arêtes and steps to the steeper rocks
at top.

Douglas Gibson Gully (DG) grade IV 600ft
Photo D/60, D/61
The difficulties are all in the final 250ft wall, the gully before
this point being an easy snow slope with perhaps one small
pitch at about mid-height. Below the top vertical wall move
onto the L wall and climb a groove in corner or the wall
further to L, both of which lead to a chimney; at top of this
move L into a scoop and so up to cornice, which may well be
crux.

Right Fork, Douglas Gibson Gully grade IV 200ft
Photo D/60, D/61, D/92
This is the far-right branch leading up to Eagle Ridge end of top wall.

Eagle Ridge (5) grade V 650ft
Photo D/60, D/61, D/70, D/71
Start a few feet up R wall of Douglas Gibson Gully. Climb obvious cleft followed by several short chimneys. The only significant features in normal winter conditions are the Tower and the summer crux, which can be avoided.

Eagle Buttress (6) grade III/IV 900ft
Photo D/61, D/72
This climb is located on the wide face between Parallel Gully A and Eagle Ridge. Start about midway between these two features. The climbing is straightforward for first 400ft to the top of a central snow scoop. Now angle up R to under steep upper wall. Take ledge R to gain three parallel V-grooves above Gully A. Climb centre groove (crux). Alternatively take L groove (harder). The climbing is now obvious and takes edge of Gully A. Finish up Gully A at top, or take steep groove just R of centre of top rocks.

Parallel Gully A (Pa) grade II/III 700ft
Photo D/60, D/73
The first 80ft ice pitch is now usually climbed. An alternative start is up easy rock on Eagle Buttress and TR up to gain gully 150ft above. Up steep snow past fork. Follow main L branch. A steep gully goes up L wall at finish, often corniced. The true R branch of the gully has been climbed, grade IV.

Parallel Buttress (7) grade V 700ft
Photo D/60, D/61, D/74
It is usual now to incorporate the lower section of buttress in this route. The obvious chimney gives the hardest climbing in this section. Above Tough-Brown Traverse difficulty may be

encountered just above 'The Necklace' and on the Tower, where aid may be required if there is a shortage of ice in groove.

Parallel Gully B (Pb) grade V 700ft
Photo D/60, D/75, D/76, D/77
Climb as directly as possible (probably easier on the L), into the chimney and follow it to the top over some difficult ice bulges, good P runners and B being found on R wall; after chimney climb directly up large ice pitch above and then move R below upper overhanging ice pitch to climb on ice groove. Above this move either R or L to top.

Tough-Brown Traverse (8) grade III 900ft
Photo D/60, D/61
Start L of Parallel Gully A and follow diagonal line to reach Tough-Brown Buttress above chimney of Parallel Gully B. Follow Great Terrace across face with some awkward steps. Continue up Ridge to top.

Tough-Brown Ridge Direct (9) grade IV 800ft
Photo D/61, D/62
Start from just inside Raeburn's Gully. A long L-sloping groove is gained via a short wall then a slabby ledge leading R. At top of groove TR R to large blocks. Now go L by flake crack and short slab TR finishes at terrace. Go up this R 150ft to gain edge of wall. Move R and pass beneath short vertical wall to reach steep groove above Raeburn's. Ascend groove to easier terrain near Backdoor Route.

Backdoor Route (Br) grade III/IV 700ft
Photo D/61, D/78
Immediately R of Tough-Brown Ridge a conspicuous system of grooves falls directly to just below bend in Raeburn's Gully. Climb from well beyond triangular smooth wall at mouth of Raeburn's. Follow the groove system throughout and gain Ridge crest approx. 150ft beneath plateau.

Raeburn's Gully (R) grade II 600ft
Photo D/60, D/61, D/62, D/80

Early in the season it may present a long, difficult ice pitch owing to spring water. There is often a very large cornice which may necessitate a steep TR to top of Tough-Brown Ridge on L. In spring a section of the cornice on the R often remains hanging after main section has fallen (invisible from below).

Scarface (10) grade IV 550ft
Photo D/61, D/62

A direct line can be made to the Amphitheatre in good conditions, especially late in the season. Take the easiest line up L, then R to gain steep chimney. This pitch and the groove above can form a continuous ice pitch to the Amphitheatre. Follow up L edge of Amphitheatre then the L of three faults above the Amphitheatre. Finish on L on the last few feet of rib.

Pinnacle Gully 1 (PG1) grade II/III 700ft
Photo D/62, D/81, D/82

This is the gully running upwards from the Mound (M, Photo D/62) to the col behind the Pinnacle. Lower climb takes a diagonal fault. TR out sharp R via snow-filled crevasse after two pitches.

Amphitheatre Route (11) grade II/III 700ft
Photo D/61, D/62

Ascend Pinnacle Gully 1 to where there is a crevasse traverse. Now climb directly a small gully followed by 50ft chimney to gain A = Amphitheatre (crux). Go up R in narrow snow gully to cornice.

Pinnacle Face (12) grade V 700ft
Photo D/60, D/61, D/83, D/84

Take one of two grooves which angle L onto face from corner of Black Spout, approx. 30ft above lowest rocks. Follow short chimney and cracks trending L. Up a few feet to corner, then onto R-hand slab, possibly aid if no ice. Continue L up slabby fault to Bay. Go up R by depression to below steep corner. Either climb corner and TR R to Route 1, or descend 15ft and go round to join Route 1 at lower level.

Route 1 (R1) grade IV 650ft
Photo D/60, D/61, D/86

Start in Black Spout, past the vertical groove in steep smooth wall beneath Springboard. Ascend groove and slab L-wards to shallow cave. Go directly up, then slant L to top of pillar (large blocks), and by 8ft wall to reach Springboard. Ascend ledges in centre, and TR into L one at 100ft. (This is the junction with Winter Face and Pinnacle Face). Follow up L fault, where initial difficulty is small steep wall. This gives way to ledges. Go up R. Easier ground is reached above with the crest reached at a point overlooking the bifurcation in the Spout. Now a wall and arête leads to Pinnacle Summit.

Route 2 (R2) grade IV 400ft
Photo D/61, D/85

From far L of large platform above fork in Black Spout, climb obvious chimney crack rising L and ending at little ridge protruding from steep gable wall, 120ft. Go down ledges L for 20ft until possible to go round corner onto face. TR horizontally to beneath steep groove of the Link. Now an angled ledge runs to the top part of a big groove. Continue TR on slab then move into groove in short descent. Ascend groove 20ft to B on big ledges, 80ft. Now the climb follows Route 1, 200ft to top.

The Stack (13) grade IV 500ft
Photo D/60, D/87

The initial section finishes at big platform 120ft up; thereafter it takes a rising line of chimneys high above face overlooking Left Hand Branch. Most parties now gain the platform by climbing the icefall on L, or from just beneath the pitch in the Branch go up zigzag cracks in slab to steep wall on R, 60ft. Go up corner in wall and above move off block, thereafter keeping R to platform. Move to base of obvious chimney, B. Up chimney for a few feet until a move L is made to narrow ledge ('handrail'). Move down ledge to platform, 30ft. (NB: It may be possible to climb this impasse and avoid the descending TR L, alternatively, a TR lower can be made to gain short chimneys.) Return R by two short chimneys to alcove above impasse. Take chimney directly ahead for another 30ft to big bollard. Move off this onto sloping shelf, then up short wall to platform. Go L then up 15ft slab to easier ground beneath final wall. Take easy terrace slanting L to short step and plateau. (NB: Moving from bollard to shelf can be crux, but possible to avoid this on R by iced-slabby fault just above and R of alcove.)

The Black Spout (BS) grade I 650ft
Photo D/60, D/67
A straightforward snow climb and the cornice seldom gives difficulty.

Black Spout, Left Branch (BSL) grade I 350ft
Photo D/61, D/79
This branch is hidden behind the Pinnacle on a frontal view of the cliffs. There is a short through route not far above the fork in summer but this fills in in winter. The Left Branch is slightly steeper than the main Spout.

Black Spout Buttress (14) grade III 850ft
Photo D/60, D/88
The lower buttress should be incorporated in a winter ascent of this route. The initial chimney usually contains an ice pitch. Turn the 30ft wall at top by R TR to gain recess at top of a gully (Western Slant). Now ascend on R of recess and go L as soon as possible to reach crest.

Gargoyle Chimney (not marked) grade III/IV 400ft
Photo D/90
This is the obvious slit in middle of upper face. The lower
chimney often offers a 100ft ice pitch. Beyond, easier ground
leads to the amphitheatre and the plateau.

Causeway Rib (not marked) grade IV 400ft
Photo D/89
This is the L rib of Gargoyle Chimney; start just L of Chimney
and follow general line of rib to top.

Gargoyle Direct (15) grade IV 500ft
Photo D/60, D/90
This route follows the rib L of West Gully. Start at terrace, or
directly from below. Above Terrace start R of shallow gully
which is R of Gargoyle Chimney and approx 30ft L of West
Gully edge. Follow up close to the shallow gully taking the
fault and chimney system above (a chockstone above a cave is
often the crux). Further difficulties are sometimes
encountered at the rising R TR beneath the Gargoyle.
Alternatively take the last pitch of Gargoyle Chimney.

West Gully (W) grade IV 600ft
Photo D/60
Climb lower icefall which usually gives one steep ice pitch of
about 80ft. Continue up over three pitches to L or central
exit.

Captions to illustrations

D/1   Coire an t-Sneachda, northern Cairngorms. To the
right, out of view, is Fiacaill Buttress. The black
circles denote climbers. AS = Aladdin's Seat. T =
Trident Gullies. A = Aladdin's Buttress.
H. MacInnes

D/2   Cairn Lochan and Fiacaill Ridge. *H. MacInnes*

D/28 Look C Gully, grade IV, Glen Clova. *G. Hunter*

D/29 B Gully Chimney, last pitch is the crux. B Gully Buttress Tower on right, Glen Clova. *G. Hunter*

D/30 Crux pitch Look C Gully, Corrie Fee, Glen Clova. *G. Hunter*

D/31 Craig of Gowal, East Face (235805). *G. Hunter*

D/32 The Gowk IV, Craig of Gowal. The traverse below the big overlap on the third pitch. *G. Hunter*

D/33 Winter Corrie of Driesh, Glen Clova. *G. Hunter*

D/34 Looking across the head of Loch Avon to Cairn Etchachan and Shelter Stone Crag. S = Shelter Stone. t = Terrace. *A. Fyffe*

D/35 The Shelter Stone Crag with part of the Castlegates Gully side of Cairn Etchachan. E = Escape line on Citadel. *R. O'Donovan*

D/36 Shelter Stone Crag from the Shelter Stone (S). E = Escape line on Citadel. *G. Strange*

D/37 Breach Gully, Shelter Stone Crag, grade IV. *G. Strange*

D/38 The lower pitches of Citadel. S = Shelter Stone. *G. Strange*

D/39 Siberia, Cairn Etchachan. *A. Fyffe*

D/40 Hell's Lum Crag, Loch Avon. *A. Fyffe*

D/41 Brimstone Grooves, Hell's Lum Crag. *A. Fyffe*

D/42 The approach to Salamander. *G. Strange*

D/43 Stag Rocks, Loch Avon; behind, the summit of Cairngorm. C = Coire Cas. d = descent route to Loch Avon. D = Diagonal Gully, a steeper descent line. B = Saddle, with Strath Nethy beyond. *H. MacInnes*

D/44 Coire of the Chockstone Gully. *G. Strange*

D/45 Bugaboo Rib, Coire of the Chockstone Gully. *G. Strange*

D/46 Cornice at top of Bugaboo Rib, Coire of the Chockstone Gully. Garbh Choire Mhor in background. *G. Strange*

D/47 The Wanderer, Coire of the Chockstone Gully. *G. Strange*

D/48 Garbh Choire Mor with Great Gully on the left.
      Pinnacle Buttress is far right on photograph.
      G. Strange
D/49 Garbh Coire Dhaidh, Braeriach. *G. Strange*
D/50 Coire Bhrochain, Braeriach. ST = Slab Terrace: b =
      Black Pinnacle. *H. MacInnes*
D/51 West Buttress, Coire Bhrochain, Braeriach.
      G. Strange
D/52 Nimus, The Ice Rib, East Buttress, Coire Bhrochain,
      Braeriach. *G. Strange*
D/53 Western Couloir, West Buttress, Coire Bhrochain,
      Braeriach. *G. Strange*
D/54 Western Couloir, West Buttress, Coire Bhrochain,
      Braeriach. *G. Strange*
D/55 Creagan a' Choire Etchachan from near Hutchison
      Hut (H). The route to Loch Etchachan and Shelter
      Stone Crag is to right of face. *H. MacInnes*
D/56 The Corridor. *G. Strange*
D/57 Bastion Direct. *G. Strange*
D/58 Flanking Ribs. *G. Strange*
D/59 Bodkin. *G. Strange*
D/60 The NE Corrie of Lochnagar. The access path from
      Spittal of Glenmuick comes in from left side of
      photograph, on other side of loch. A =
      Amphitheatre. *H. MacInnes*
D/61 The cliffs of Lochnagar with Black Spout Pinnacle
      on right, (bsp). *H. MacInnes*
D/62 The bottom of Raeburn's Gully with Scarface on left
      Pinnacle Gully on right. A = Amphitheatre. *G. Strange*
D/63 Shallow Gully, Lochnagar. *G. Strange*
D/64 Giant's Head Chimney, Lochnagar. *G. Strange*
D/65 Giant's Head Chimney, Lochnagar. *G. Strange*
D/66 Polyphemus Gully, Lochnagar. *G. Strange*
D/67 Black Spout, Lochnagar. *G. Strange*
D/68 Shadow Buttress B, Lochnagar. *G. Hunter*
D/69 Bell's Route, Shadow Buttress B, Lochnagar.
      G. Strange

D/1

SUMMIT OF CAIRN LOCHAN

COIRE AN LOCHAIN

R B 4

FIACAILL RIDGE

COIRE AN T-SNEACHDA

D/2

D/3

COIRE AN LOCHAIN

FIACAILL RIDGE

R B

FIACAILL COULOIR

D/4

D/6

JEAN'S HUT

GS

C

YG

1 2 3   4   5   6 7

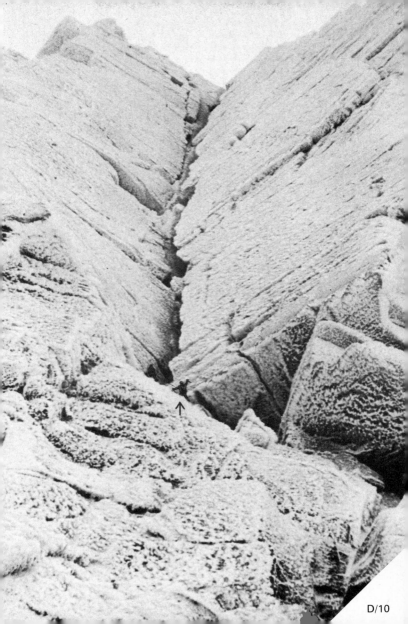

D/12

D/13

D/15

D/17

D/19

Md

cc

cc

Md

D/21

NW

C

cc

SE

Md

D/25

BG

1 2 3

T

D/27

D/29

D/30

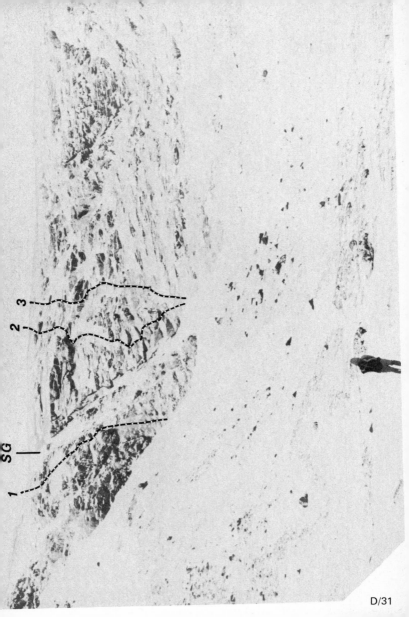

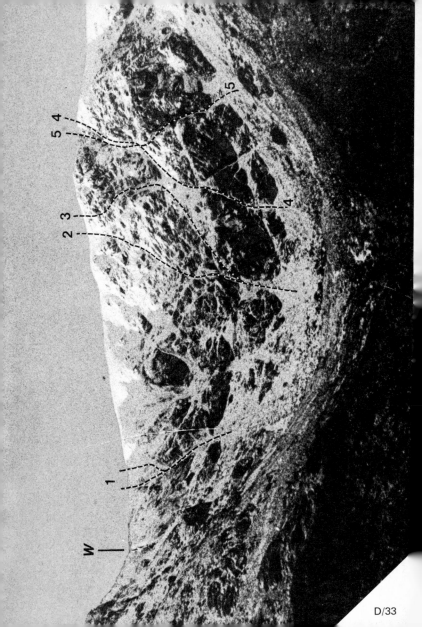

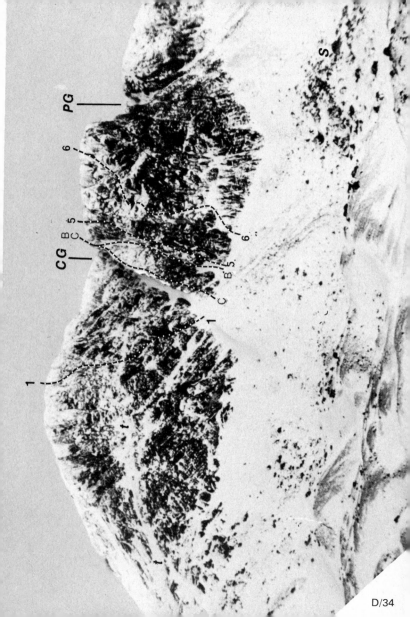

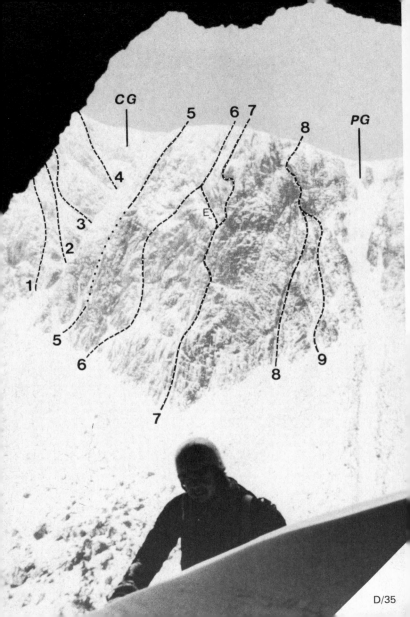

D/35

D/36

D/37

S

D/38

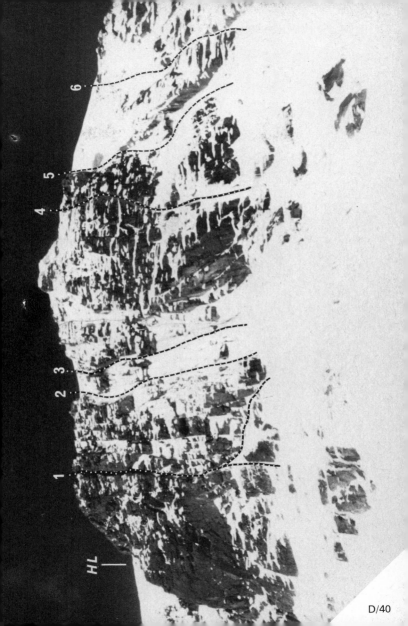

HL

1
2
3
4
5
6

D/40

D/41

D/42

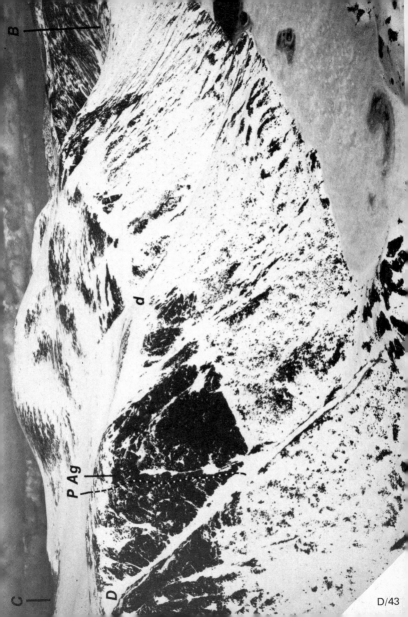

D/43

SC

C

1

2 3

4

1

2

3

4

D/44

D/45

D/47

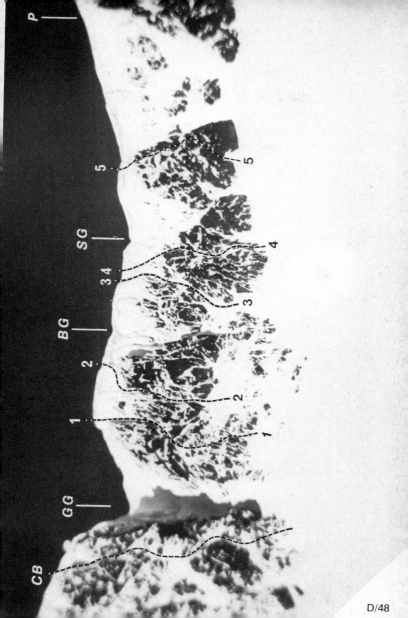

D/48

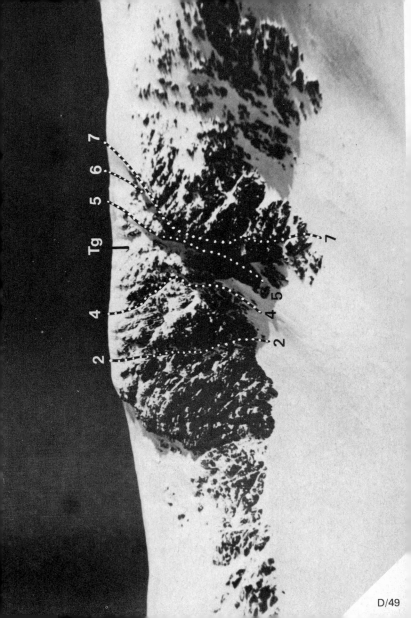

D/49

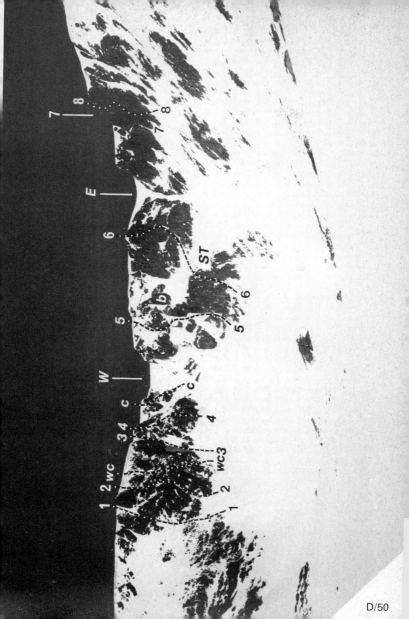

D/50

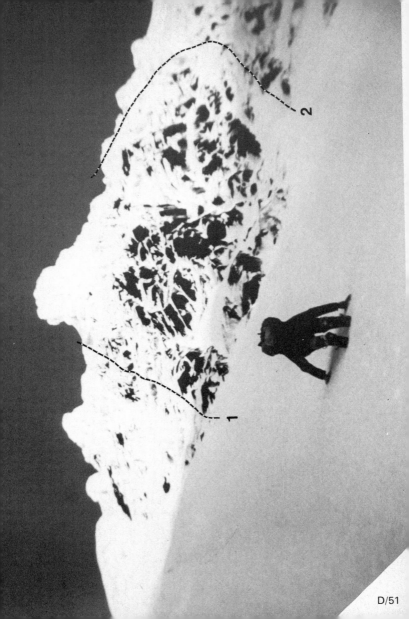

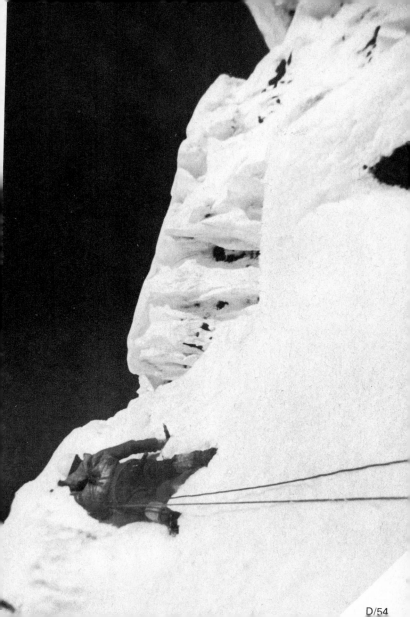

D/54

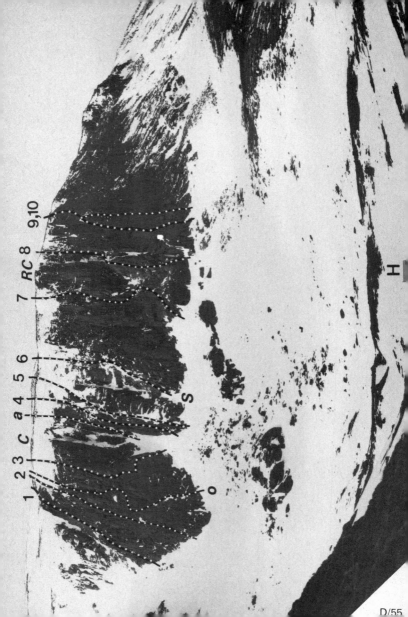

D/55

D/56

D/57

D/58

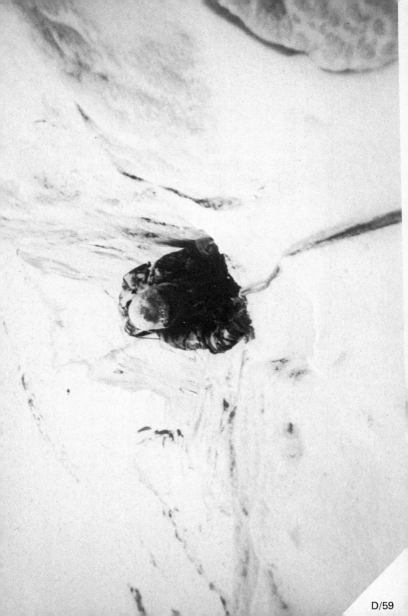

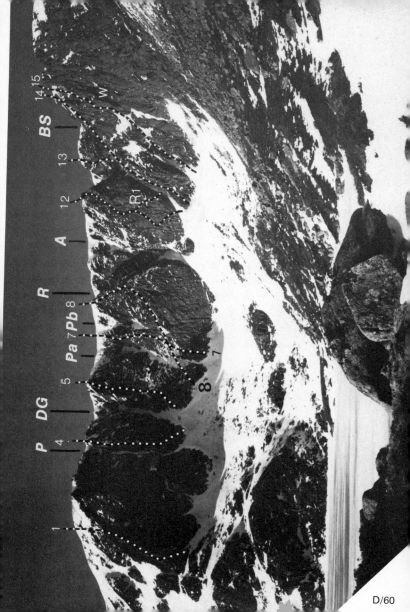

D/60

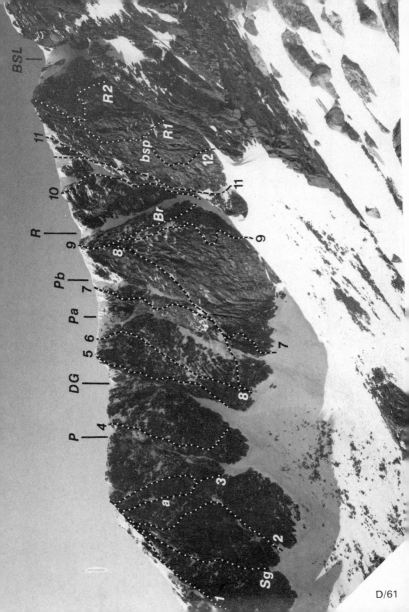

BSL

R2

R1

bsp

12

11

11

10

Br

9

R

9

8

Pb

7

Pa

5 6

DG

P

4

a

3

8

7

Sg

2

1

D/61

D/63

D/66

D/68

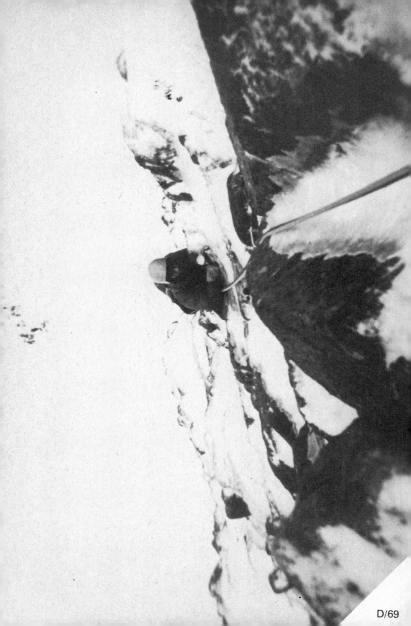

D/71

D/72

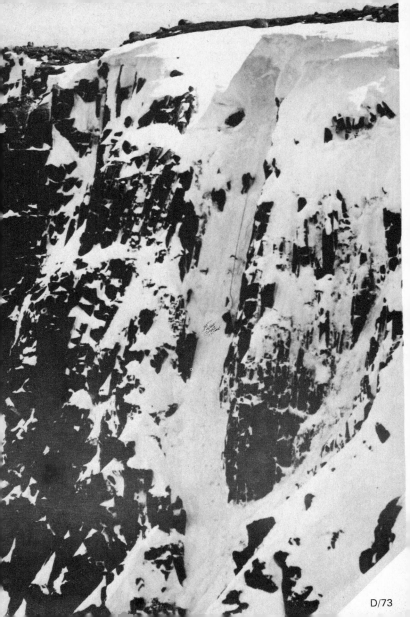

D/74

D/75

D/78

D/80

D/81

D/84

D/85

D/86

D/87

D/90

Ben Nevis (4406ft, 1343m)

Map: OS Tourist map, Ben Nevis and Glencoe, 1 in to 1 mile

The 'Ben', as it is known to climbers, gives winter climbing of an alpine character coupled with the possibility of severe weather and sharing with the rest of Scottish peaks north of latitude 56° a shortage of daylight hours. The main climbing is on the NE face of the mountain and one approach is up the Allt a'Mhuilinn from the golf course on the Fort William–Inverness road. This is boggy and sometimes the forestry road from Torlundy can be used to a parking place close by the small dam on the Allt a'Mhuilinn (check with Forestry Commission). Alternatively, leave Achintee Farm on the east side of the River Nevis and take the Tourist Path as far as the half-way lochan (Lochan Meall an t-Suidhe). Here a narrow path breaks off leftwards to skirt the lochan on its east side and, after crossing the remains of an old deer fence, slants down into the Allt a'Mhuilinn under the shadow of Carn Dearg, the first and most northerly of the Ben buttresses. The Charles Ingles Clark Hut at the foot of the cliffs is open only to Scottish Mountaineering Club members or members of affiliated clubs.

The two principal features of the face of the Ben are Tower Ridge, near the middle, and on the left the steeply rising North East Buttress. Between is a galaxy of gullies, subsidiary buttresses and faces which offer a great assortment of climbs for all tastes. Beyond North East Buttress is the Little Brenva Face which, late in the winter, offers sunshine as well as alpine type climbing. At its base lies Coire Leis, bounded by the curve of Carn Mor Dearg Arête, an airy and often icy edge in winter. Here a series of abseil posts (MR 171711) leads down in 50ft intervals to the security of the coire floor. This descent route from the summit of the Ben is one of the most popular. Steer 130° (true) from the summit shelter for 400 yards, then go due east, keeping the route markers to your left as you go down from the summit, to gain the arête.

On the summit is a bivouac shelter. It is for emergency use only. Remember, if you use it, someone may have to come up to check if you are reported overdue. It is much better to make an early start for the climbs than risk an uncomfortable bivouac and the displeasure of friends or the local rescue team!

In the event of poor visibility or severe weather, it is usually better and safer to descend Gully 4 (marker at top). Gully 3 can also be used and this can be usually identified by the small pinnacle at the top. If in doubt return to the tourist track and on the way down be careful not to descend into the top of Five Finger Gully.

Route Major (1) grade III 1000ft
Photo E/4, E/5

This long climb involves considerable route finding. Start at lowest point of rocks and follow route line on illustrations. Frostbite is crossed at the broad snow ledge and the upper section of the route, though looking formidable, is straightforward with a number of exposed TR.

Frostbite (2) grade III 900ft
Photo E/4

Start from same snow bay as Slalom and take ice groove to R to reach 400ft snowfield. Up this R and cross rock ridge below nose of Central Spur proper to reach further snow slopes trending R under Spur. Go out R on to North East Buttress on these and finish by Man Trap. (See North East Buttress.)

Slalom (3) grade II 900ft
Photo E/4

Route rises towards Central Spur, zigzags to avoid rock walls. It is separated from Frostbite by rock ridge and runs parallel.

Below spur TR 100ft L, easy snow slope leads to final rocks overlooking Cresta Gully and just L of Central Spur (rocks, crux), easy climbing from top.

Cresta Climb (4) grade II 900ft
Photo E/4
Start to L of rocky spur, and 100ft R of Bob-run. Iced rocks (or ice) are climbed to reach broad snowshelf. A small gully leads up R side of shelf to couloir. Follow couloir to top in ice basin. TR up R to easy snow slope to finish.

Bob-run (5) grade II 400ft
Photo E/4
Start almost level with Carn Mor Dearg Arête Col. Route takes a couloir at L side of face. Start to R of buttress and climb 100ft of ice or iced rocks to gain couloir. In a further 100ft the route trends L. Two variations above, with usually one ice pitch in each.

North East Buttress (NEB) grade III 1000ft
Photo E/4, E/6, E/17, E/25
Gain First Platform (usually by rising TR from E). On the steeper rocks of the crest above TR ledge on R to gully, leading back L to gain Second Platform. Take easiest route to Man Trap. This can be turned on R by short descent and TR to scoop. This leads to base to steep corner, which can also be hard (it may be better to move down and L to near top of Man Trap; a shallow chimney goes up L of ridge crest on easier terrain). It is also possible to turn the Man Trap by descending and moving E then up.

Slingsby's Chimney (S) grade II/III 400ft
Photo E/6
This gives a good direct approach to First Platform on North East Buttress from west. To R of slabby rocks of the nose leading to First Platform is a prominent gully fault. If North East Buttress is not followed above a descent can be made into Coire Leis.

Raeburn's 18-Minute Route (not marked) grade II 450ft
Photo E/6
Start 20ft L of Slingsby's Chimney and up L wall of gully.

Platform Rib (not marked) grade IV 700ft
Photo E/6
50ft R of Slingsby's Chimney is a deep chimney. The rock rib forming L wall is climbed after ascending a few feet in chimney. Go up rib mostly on rib (short sections in chimney). An easy chimney at top leads to North East Buttress, 100ft above First Platform.

Minus Three Gully (-3) grade IV 520ft
Photo E/6, E/7
Ascend to foot of gully; follow by steep snow and ice to reach deep cave at 100ft. Exit L up ice wall to gain groove leading to bottom of next pitch, B, 80ft. Up groove above; finish by short difficult wall at 80ft then continue on snow to B, 130ft. A 50ft ice pitch leads to mixed (easier) climbing and the crest of North East Buttress. NB: Escape can be made from below each pitch onto Platform Rib.

Minus Two Buttress (not marked) grade V 900ft
Photo E/6
From 40ft L of Minus Two Gully, climb L on iced slab for 100ft. Now go up and R to reach open corner. Up this and over ledge to P belay (150ft). Follow up corner then a snow crest (150ft). TR L across snow ramp to reach iced gully (150ft). Up gully to snowfield (150ft). Take narrow gully (210ft total) to arrive at crest of North East Buttress.

Minus Two Gully (-2) grade V 900ft
Photo E/6, E/8
Follow snow up to bulging ice pitch some 30ft high. Mixed climbing up a groove and overhang. The chimney above the overhang can be used as ST, B. Now go L on delicate slab TR to reach upper chimney line. Follow this to steeper chimneys above which are climbed by line of weakness. Now take bed

of gully to fork. Climb L fork up icy chimneys to crest of
buttress.

Minus One Buttress (not marked) grade V 850ft
Photo E/6
Start at lowest rocks of Minus One Buttress. Climb 75ft to
corner and exit this R to snow-covered glacis, 85ft. Climb
shallow groove in wall above to detached block at 20ft.
Ascend this by crack on R, then up short walls, trending L to
niche, 65ft. Go R and up easily to top of big plinth. Step L into
icy groove and up this for 75ft to overhang. Now go R (to join
Minus One Direct) onto nose above overhang and climb to
ledge. At the R end of this is an undercut groove. Climb this
until ramp above is gained up R, finishing at block on
platform, 100ft. Climb up to crack, climb an overhang, and
back into and up wide crack above to the Meadow. ST at large
detached flake, 85ft. Up grooves on L side of gully to small
ST, 60ft. Follow up corner until possible to TR L across loose
wall into a niche, 70ft. Keep going L onto crest of buttress.
Up slabs and cracks to great terrace, 140ft. Ascend to top of
40ft flake, then up crest to poised pedestal, 90ft. Take
narrow arête beyond to reach North East Buttress above
Second Platform.

Minus One Gully (-1) grade V 1000ft
Photo E/6
Climb direct to ice wall and cave below main gully overhang.
Turn this by tension TR to L edge (or climb direct). Bypass
next overhang on L. A steep ice wall and corner leads to snow
bay. Now take L of two grooves to its end and TR R to gain
other groove. Go up to L mantelshelf exit onto crest of Minus
One Buttress. Take crest to top.

Astronomy (not marked) grade V 955ft
Photo E/6, E/9, E/10
Start 100ft up from foot of Minus One Gully. Up twin cracks
to snow shelves leading L. Follow these and deep groove until

return R can be made to large L-sloping corner. Climb this and exit R by wide shallow flake chimney. Go up, then R into thin ice groove and trend back L by walls and grooves. Continue this L trend under steep upper rocks until near top, where a short descent is made into steep chimney at top of Minus One Gully. Climb this to crest of North East Buttress.

The Orion Face, Direct (Od) grade V 1400ft
Photo E/6, E/11, E/12, E/15
Take the direct line which starts from the broad ledge of Slav Route. This is reached after 100ft of ice climbing. Follow an ice groove to PB below a roof. Make a L TR to the Basin. Snow and ice climbing leads to base of second slab rib. This is turned by ice wall on R. L-slanting ice and snow grooves lead to snow slopes below last tower of North East Buttress. Ice grooves lead to summit slopes.

Slav Route (SL) grade V 1480ft
Photo E/6, E/15
Take groove just L of Zero Gully. Go L round ice hose at top to PB (170ft). Take a steep depression up L. Move R close to rock wall, then back L and over ice bulges to P B (170ft crux). (This point is level with the Basin.) Continue in R-rising line to B beneath snow arête overlooking Zero Gully (180ft). Now up grooves and steps for four pitches, close, but above Zero. Gain a point beneath wide square-cut chimney just R of obvious buttress. (It is possible to enter Zero here.) TR over groove and wall for 100ft, then ascend steep groove to reach bollard B (190ft). Follow groove on L, below wall to gain crest of North East Buttress well L of top of Zero Gully.

Zero Gully (Z) grade V 1000ft
Photo E/6, E/9, E/10, E/13, E/14, E/17
First 400ft very steep, few belays (dead man B may be useful) which makes this a potentially dangerous climb. Upper section of climb is easy.

East Face, Observatory Ridge (not marked) grade IV

550ft

Photo E/10

Below and R of Zero Gully an obvious groove slants L up East Face of Observatory Ridge. Take this to crest of ridge over several ice bulges.

Observatory Ridge, Ordinary Route (Or) grade III

900ft

Photo E/6, E/17, E/18

The most difficult of the classic ridges of Ben Nevis. The lowest buttress usually gives the hardest problems. Gain a shelf on L side one-third way up this buttress then slant R to crest. Difficulties can be turned above this and Zero Gully can be climbed for the last 500ft if time is short.

Hadrian's Wall (H) grade IV 800ft

Photo E/19

Up snow and ice to pointed block and follow iced grooves to steep snow bay under vertical wall. The slab TRs can be awkward and the following chimney is often heavily iced. Above, a shallow scoop leads to the plateau.

Point Five Gully (.5) grade V 1000ft

Photo E/6, E/17, E/19, E/22, E/23, E/24

Up steep ice-covered slab to bolt B (in place) on L wall; 40–100ft. Up to groove on L of ice bulge. Surmount bulge on R; 60ft for ST and P B 25ft higher. Difficult ice bulge followed by vertical pitch in narrowing chimney to ST and P B (in place) at foot of tight chimney; 60ft. Up chimney, then easier climbing (apart from 10ft bulge) to ST and P B; 60ft. Up to foot of cave pitch. Bolt B (in place on L wall); 35ft. Climb a steepening ice pitch; vertical at top. Difficult exit to snow slope, P B on R; 45ft. Easily up snow 100ft; awkward ice-covered rocks climbed L to R. 500ft of climbing involving one small steep pitch and a strenuous ice chimney leads to top.

Left Edge Route, Observatory Buttress (L) grade v
420ft

Photo E/19

Start at base of Point Five Gully and just above lowest rocks.
Ascend extreme L edge to small snow bay. B at cracked blocks
on R (100ft). Continue up the L of two grooves. Move out R
(difficult) then up R one to P B (160ft). Up icefall direct to
Terrace (160ft), poor B. Go R to join normal buttress route.

Rubicon Wall (R) grade IV 400ft

Photo E/19

Start 50ft from L edge of buttress and climb to large ledge
30ft (sometimes covered). From L end up rock rib to ledge
and block B, 60ft. Go R, climb into groove which goes to big
ledge and B, 40ft. TR R 40ft to gully. Climb this, and move R to
large block B, 90ft. Continue TR R past small buttress to V
corner. Go out R and up to finish by corner and rib, B 60ft.
Follow corner/rib to ledge, B 20ft. From R end of ledge go up,
slanting L to higher ledge and thin crack and groove to B,
60ft. Climb corner on L to sloping ledges and B, 40ft. Up
grooves then R onto rib and up to ledge. Up blocks to recess,
go R to small ledge, 80ft. Go up R into corner with big block.
Up this to easier terrain.

Good Friday Climb (F) grade III 500ft

Photo E/6, E/18, E/19

Start of climb is at head of Observatory Gully and below
Gardyloo Gully (see Gardyloo Gully for start). To L a snow
shelf runs out to top of Observatory Buttress and a gully is
taken for 240ft until blocked by wall. Go R then back L up
further gully system to top. Upper section, which is steep, can
be hard when icy.

Gardyloo Gully (Gg) grade III 400ft

Photo E/6, E/17, E/18, E/19

Conditions and difficulty depend on build up of snow; most
pitches are usually covered and it is easy as far as the through

route – there is sometimes a tunnel under the chockstone – but usually the R of this has to be climbed. Continue up on steep snow or ice to cornice (often double) which can be awkward.

Gardyloo Buttress, Smith's Route (Gb) grade v 400ft
Photo E/17, E/19
Start directly beneath lower end of slanting grooves. Up ice groove 120ft to bottom of main grooves, PB. TR up and L across lower groove to easier section. Go up to steeper ground, up R on high-angled ice to reach L edge of upper slab groove. Climb this to bottom of upper funnel, 150ft (PB possible at mid-height). Up funnel to plateau.

Tower Gully (Tg) grade I 350ft
Photo E/17, E/18, E/35
Usually an even snow slope in winter, though there can be ice in severe conditions. Cornice sometimes has to be tunnelled.

Tower Ridge (Tr) grade III 1900ft
Photo E/16, E/17, E/18, E/19, E/25, E/29, E/35
Climb the eastern gully leading to Douglas Gap. This is marked on photograph. It is not always easy to locate gully in misty weather as its base merges with the broad rocky slope, but the bay should be found. From gap an easy chimney slants L to give access to ridge crest. Ridge is fairly level and narrow and steepens to small pitch with overhanging wall. Climb up to and along ledge running R. Easy scrambling above. Two small gaps are crossed. 160ft beyond second gap, base of Little Tower is reached. Normal route is up rocks on L. Easy to Great Tower base. The ridge crest goes to its NE corner. Keep to E, on ledge (Eastern Traverse), to foot of through route formed by big block, up to steep easy rocks on R to summit of Tower. Descend to Tower Gap, cross and follow to steep small buttress, turned on R by a chimney, or easier rock W. Care should be taken at the exposed section above Echo Wall at the Little Tower. The Eastern Traverse is the obvious ledge running L of onset of Great Tower (see photos E/15, E/18).

Vanishing Gully (V) grade IV 350ft
Photo E/19, E/26
100yds beyond Douglas Gap West Chimney is a big bay. The gully, not very defined in its lower reaches, starts here. It gets more obvious higher. The start is usually a 200ft icefall and above steepens into bulges. Beyond it emerges onto a big snowfield and it is possible to exit onto Tower Ridge crest below Little Tower.

Italian Climb (I) grade IV 600ft
Photo E/19, E/28
There is a deep gully with an obvious two-tier rib on L, on W side of Tower Ridge. This climb follows the gully with two main ice pitches followed by a slanting TR R across face to reach crest of Tower Ridge under Little Tower, or climb direct.

Garadh Gully (g) grade II 400ft
Photo E/17, E/18, E/19
This gully gives (usually) two steep ice pitches, 50ft and 40ft. Start just above and R of Italian Climb.

Pinnacle Buttress of the Tower (PB) grade III 500ft
Photo E/29
From the Garadh ascend by L up shallow snow gully about 150ft, then R along easy ledge. Above, crest of buttress rises in steep ridge with easier rocks either side. Route goes R of crest over snow and ice-covered rock. A snow-filled groove is climbed; 60ft approx. Then R TR of 40ft to another groove followed straight up until easy rocks lead L to top of buttress, below Great Tower. This part goes up midway between crest of Buttress and Glover's Chimney.

Glover's Chimney, Tower Gap (GC) grade III 450ft
Photo E/29
This is Tower Gap W Chimney. Starts from Garadh na Ciste to R of Pinnacle Buttress route and goes directly to Tower Gap via the narrow gully. Choose the line of least resistance.

Crux is usually final chimney and can be climbed on L or R walls. 150ft of rope recommended due to lack of suitable ST. Climb finishes at Tower Gap.

Gully 2 Buttress (1) grade II 400ft
Photo E/31
Up steep snow and occasionally iced rocks to shelf below steep upper wall. A short hard ice pitch leads to easier snow above.

Gully 2 (2) grade I/II 400ft
Photo E/31, E/35
This gully is situated between the cliffs which merge with Tower Ridge and the Comb. It cuts deeply into the cliffs. The climb is easier when banked-up with snow; if not, the Great Pitch can present difficulties. There is often a large cornice.

Comb Gully Buttress (c) grade III 450ft
Photo E/35
Normally a big column of ice forms on R wall, beyond start of Comb Gully and before Gully 2 narrows. Start below this and climb slightly R to gain snow basin. Follow groove from L side of this up slanting R ramp. Now the upper half of obvious curving chimney is gained (crux). Exit on L.

Comb Gully (Cg) grade III 450ft
Photo E/18, E/31, E/32, E/35
Early in winter this gully may be hard with steep ice in upper section.

Green Gully (g) grade III/IV 400ft
Photo E/35
This gully flanks the Comb on the Carn Dearg side. Near the start there is an ice chimney, on the L are the steep cliffs of the Comb. Shortly after this gully steepens (steep walls either side) and some easier pitches lead to 60ft ice pitch, followed

by another steep ice wall. Next section fairly easy to bottom of
final difficulties, a pitch usually climbed up R corner of wall.
Finish up snow scoop.

Gully 3 Buttress (not marked) grade II/III 500ft
Photo E/35
An obvious buttress projects into coire on L and under
narrow part of Gully 3. Two-thirds way up buttress is an
obvious platform. From big snow bay under prow of buttress
climb to platform. Grooves lead up L, and a steep corner
gives a good finish.

Gully 3 (3) grade I 300ft
Photo E/35
This is an easy gully rising from Coire na Ciste. No pitches,
but quite steep. Top section is divided by pinnacle (visible
from hut). L side is easier. This gully together with Gully 4
provide good descent routes, but if in doubt, in bad visibility,
descend by tourist path.

South Gully (S) grade II 400ft
Photo E/35
Climb from foot of narrow section of Gully 3, level with
lowest part of Gully 3 Buttress. Go to the R up prominent
steep angled ledge to foot of gully. Gully goes back up L.
Finish near highest part of Creag Coire na Ciste. Cornice can
be difficult.

Central Gully (C3) grade III 600ft
Photo E/35
Start at lowest part of crag, follow snow slopes L of rocky rib
to reach the L of two parallel chimneys, which run up steep
central wall. Climb this for 120ft before crossing to R gully.
This leads into final runnel, cornice.

North Gully (n) grade II 350ft

Photo E/35

To the L of Gully 4 and just below a thin steep black buttress is a couloir. Crux is where couloir narrows and steepens, and vertical ice pitch 12–14ft is climbed (this pitch can be 100ft sometimes). Moderate snow leads to foot of black buttress. Keep to R past this and snow slope leads to summit.

Gully 4 (4) grade I 400ft

Photo E/25, E/35

See location from photograph: one of the easiest of the gullies, though sometimes there is a cornice. An easy descent route (at present, marker at top of gully).

Gully 4 Buttress (b) grade I/II 400ft

Photo E/25

Start above wide ledge R of narrowing in Gully 4. This ledge leads out onto South Trident Buttress. Go up L slanting chimney to easier ground, 200ft. Follow over rocks and snow to steeper final rocks, various lines.

Jubilee Gully (J) grade II/III 800ft

Photo E/25

The climb lies in the rear of the recess below and R of South Trident Buttress and is a short way from the corrie floor. The gully forks a short way up. Take R fork of Jubilee (L for Central Gully – see below). Follow up R over easy slabs for 250ft to beneath steep corner and crack. Up this for 10ft, TR R over blocks to B. Climb slabs above, 40ft, and then snow for 40ft to short chimney and slab. This leads to snow slope in 100ft. Above, the upper buttress can be seen on L. Climb buttress crest (two pitches) 240ft. Easier to top.

Central Gully: From fork go up to ice pitch, this can be turned on L to regain upper snow bay. The upper buttress can be bypassed on L by a gully, then regained above steeper section and taken to top.

Moonlight Gully (m) grade I/II 500ft
Photo E/25

L of Gully 5, Moonlight Gully Buttress separates Gully 5 from
Moonlight Gully. The gully is direct and narrow.

Gully 5 (5) grade I 1500ft
Photo E/25, E/35

A straightforward snow climb.

The Curtain (C) grade IV 300ft
Photo E/35, E/36, E/37

This is the big slab-corner in upper L side of Great Buttress.
In winter it forms a great curtain of ice.

Route II Direct (R2) grade V 750ft
Photo E/35, E/38

Start just L of The Shadow. Up centre of slab to small ledge.
TR 4ft R to a wall, then by a small angled corner to TR L to ST.
Go up small black crack to flake B, 100ft. Follow straight up
to big block below groove, 50ft. Ascend groove, then TR R,
round arête, to reach shattered ledge, 30ft. Climb bulge
above to gain easier ground and B close to chimney to Route
I. Climb chimney for 40ft, TR slab on R to small ST and B, 20ft.
Go up R for two pitches, 30ft and 50ft, to gain a big flake
beneath large overhangs. Go over flake, TR it for 20ft then
climb to rock rib (thread B). TR buttress R for two pitches:
100ft and 30ft to platform on buttress edge. Go up edge of
buttress, 100ft, and gain groove which is taken mainly on R
wall for two pitches, 70ft and 40ft, so gaining the crest of
buttress.

The Shadow (Sh) grade V 800ft
Photo E/35, E/39, E/40, E/41

Go up crack a few feet R of direct start of Route II. Up crack
then TR R to B, 90ft. Climb block above, round corner to gain
small groove to ledge, 40ft. Up wall above, go R to enter
groove (grassy in summer), 90ft. Climb groove until it

widens, then TR R 30ft to block Bs, 120ft. Go up then TR L beneath a slab to break through overlap; follow on to small corner, 130ft. Climb – trending R – TR across ice to groove (grassy) of Centurion, 130ft. Go up R to B in corner (grassy) on buttress crest, 120ft. Up R wall of corner and TR L across further slab to ledge, B, 80ft. Climb groove above, 80ft.

Shield Direct (Sd) grade V/VI 970ft
Photo E/35

This climb starts at the prominent streak of ice coming from the foot of chimney section of Shield; continues up chimney to top of flake (where chimney ends) then takes the face above, trending L to crest of buttress where it joins Route II. It takes Route II for the last pitch. Start at foot of ice groove directly below chimney of Shield to ST on R, 80ft. Climb the two steep sections above to large ledge below chimney of Shield, 100ft. Continue up ice chimney followed by steep ice to a cave, ST on L, 100ft. Steep ice grooves lead to easier climbing in wider chimney, 120ft. Follow on same line to top of chimney/flake (junction with Evening Wall) 130ft. Move up L onto flake, cross the bulge above, trending R on thin ice and continue by easiest line to ledges, 150ft. Trend up R to gain slanting ledge which is followed L-wards to edge of buttress, 110ft. Continue up arête to top (Route II) 180ft.

Waterfall Gully, Left Route (K) grade V 800ft
Photo E/42, E/43

Start 10ft L of Waterfall Gully and follow steep groove line with short vertical section at 30ft (120ft). It is now possible to enter Waterfall Gully, but a short (50ft) pitch leads to foot of easy-angled ramp which goes up R to foot of a big flake (on Evening Wall route, not described). An obvious steep ice smear leads to foot of chimney. Climb this to ledges and a R trending TR 100ft. (NB: It is also possible to climb chimney, easier.) Follow along TR line over exposed icy bulges to second of two grooves. Take this to large ledge, (120ft). Now take the ledge R to B, (100ft). Climb over ice slabs and ledges to finish on Ledge Route (150ft).

Waterfall Gully (6) grade III 700ft
Photo E/42, E/44
This gully is just R of Great Buttress. First section is usually an ice pitch (steep). The gully above is straightforward with awkward slabby exit into large basin. Easiest exit from snow basin is up easy ridge on L or finish via 1, 2, or 3.

Raeburn's Buttress, Ordinary Route (5) grade III 600ft
Photo E/42
This route goes up gully on S side, climbed for 200ft. The gully divides here and encloses a further buttress. Up R fork, for 100ft (narrowing) to a cave, ST chockstone, B. R wall is ascended and further similar wall, leading to crack. Reach crest of buttress on R, follow for 200ft to top. Last pitch is steep edge going to level knife edge. (Can be avoided, TR R into corner.)

Colando Gully (1) grade I 600ft
Photo E/42
The left-hand gully, no difficulties.

Arch Gully (2) grade II/III 600ft
Photo E/42
This gully has big arch block half way up, steep.

Surprise Gully (3) grade III 550ft
Photo E/42
This leads by broken rocks to a shoulder and by ice groove on L.

South Castle Gully (SC) grade I/II 700ft
Photo E/35, E/42
The long gully between the Castle and Raeburn's Buttress. If one pitch gives difficulty, climb on L wall.

The Castle (C) grade II/III 700ft
Photo E/42
A bulging wall at the base may be awkward in winter, or covered in avalanche debris. Climb direct. The upper rocks are climbed by a gully, slabs, a chimney and another shallow gully, all in middle of buttress. This leads to steep wall. Go up R over snow covered slabs to top. (NB: Sometimes avalanche danger at slabs.)

North Castle Gully (NC) grade I/II 700ft
Photo E/25, E/35, E/42
Steeper than South Castle, with several chockstone pitches. These can cover to give uniform slope.

Castle Ridge (CR) grade II 1000ft
Photo E/42
This is the easiest of the big ridges. Start just below start of North Castle Gully, or lower down as illustrated. By the higher start the rocks of ridge crest just above the little gully offer the only unavoidable difficulty. Keep to the R above.

Creagh Meaghaidh, Coire Ardair
Map: OS No. 34, Fort Autustus, 1:50,000

On the north side of the road between Spean Bridge and Newtonmore lies Creagh Meaghaidh. From Aberarder Farm on Loch Lagganside it is just short of four miles to Coire Ardair and the south-facing cliffs of Creagh Meaghaidh. Situated between the Cairngorms and the west, it often has good snow conditions when it is poor elsewhere. The stratum of the rock is horizontal and it tends to hold a lot of snow. Located at the head of the Inner Coire is a col named the Window. From here is the easiest route leading to the summit of the mountain, which at 3700ft (1128m) is approx. one mile back from the corrie edge.

The path to the mountain goes from Aberarder Farm through a gate and across a field to gain a good path beyond a drystone dyke. This rises rightwards to take a high line into the valley through the woods, following the true left of the stream. It takes two hours to reach the base of the climbs and the path (usually snow covered in winter) continues to the Window.

Descent: In good visibility the best way down is Bellevue Buttress. This ridge can be followed down towards the farm. Alternatively, Easy Gully or the line to the Window can be taken. In bad conditions many climbers have lost their way on this mountain and particular care should be taken; use map and compass if in doubt. There is a first-aid box and stretcher in the shelter in Coire Ardair close to the path.

Raeburn's Gully (RG) grade II 1200ft
Photo E/46

A good introduction to Coire Ardair. Gully trends L-wards below face of Pinnacle Buttress (at fairly high angle). Sometimes a straightforward ice pitch near top (occasionally cornice difficulties). Variations possible to L in upper section.

Apollyon Ledge (a) grade II/III 1300ft
Photo E/46

The second part of girdle TR of Coire Ardair. Crossed from Raeburn's Gully 300ft below plateau, towards Easy Gully. Spectacular climbing especially at 1000ft where ledge almost disappears (obvious rockfall), with only a horizontal slit in otherwise holdless wall. After ledge a further 600ft remain across upper slopes of Easy Gully to base of Post Face.

Ritchie's Gully (1) grade IV 500ft
Photo E/46

This is L parallel gully, TR first 200ft of Apollyon Ledge, then gully usually has three further ice pitches. Exit R of cornice.

Direct Start (if combined with Ritchie's) grade IV 210ft
Photo E/46, E/48
Climb steep corner to huge ice roof, P B; 80ft. TR up R then
up direct to Apollyon Ledge; 130ft. Continue up Ritchie's
Gully to plateau.

Smith's Gully (2) grade V 600ft
Photo E/46, E/49
The R-hand parallel gully. Normally an almost complete
scoop of steep ice. On first ascent three P used for protection,
(long run-outs). Note: First pitch after Apollyon Ledge has
now been climbed direct (crux).

1959 Face Route (3) grade IV 1500ft
Photo E/46
This takes prominent depression trending L up face of
Buttress. Start just R of lowest rocks. Follow depression
slanting L after 200ft. This develops into a shallow gully, and
above, a series of chimneys. Exit gully 150ft under the base of
first chimney and TR L 200ft to gain base of L-slanting
chimney groove with prominent chockstone. Follow groove
300ft to big snow ledges in centre of face. Another gully
develops here, going L to end 200ft under summit of
buttress. The base of gully is barred by icefall, turned on R by
rock wall. Gully is now followed (one ice pitch) to crest of
buttress.

Easy Gully (EG) grade I 1500ft
Photo E/46
Easiest route in Coire Ardair. Situated behind Pinnacle
Buttress and slants up L to plateau. Bottom part of gully is
narrow trough and upper half open snow slope (no cornice
difficulties). Many variations possible on L of main gully. Can
be used as route of descent from plateau.

The Last Post (LP) grade IV 800ft
Photo E/46

The L of prominent winter lines on the Post Face. Start about halfway up Easy Gully on L edge of impressive icefall. On first ascent, the steep angle compelled short steep TR to R. This and following 20ft of almost vertical ice was crux. Snowfield then steepened to second big icefall 200ft from bottom. Two more 60ft ice pitches on R-hand side followed. Easy until another 100ft icefall (avoided by hidden shelf on L) which led to upper amphitheatre just under plateau.

The South Post (SP) grade III 1500ft
Photo E/46

First ice pitch can be bypassed by L-rising TR from base of Centre Post across snowfield on lower section of the Central Pillar. Directly up couloir, climb 100ft ice pitch, go between narrow walls. Spectacular ice pitch of direct route is by-passed steeply on L before rejoining true line of gully. Follow this with one ice pitch to plateau.

The South Post Direct (SP) grade IV 1200ft
Photo E/46, E/50

Climb both first and third pitches direct (avoided on ordinary route). Steep first pitch (tapering icefall). In thick snow, there may be only steep snow and bergschrund. Third pitch climbed from bottom L to top R.

Post Horn Gallop (4) grade III 2000ft
Photo E/46

This forms third part of girdle TR of the Coire. Post Face is crossed diagonally from L to R. Up first pitch of Last Post, move R to narrow ledge going into South Post under its second big pitch. Slightly up, then awkwardly to wide snow ledge circling Central Pillar. Ledge turns into Centre Post under great ice pitch. Cross now by TR of ordinary route, and follow on true diagonal line to impressive (easy) balcony crossing high above little upper enclosure of North Post. 500ft to upper snow basin of Staghorn Gully.

The Central Pillar (5) grade IV 1500ft

Photo E/46

Buttress between south and Centre Posts (suitable when Posts liable to avalanche). Steep pitch from Easy Gully to steep snowfield. Above, a diagonal TR to L is made and L side of Buttress followed to prominent ledge crossing buttress at 1000ft. Climb 100ft arête (the R edge of barrier wall above is crux), and snowfield on R of crest of buttress before crossing to L and ending L of final bulge.

The Centre Post (CP) grade III 1500ft

Photo E/46

During most winters, lower 1000ft is steep snow slope, with several short ice pitches. Two-thirds up gully is the impressive ice pitch of the Centre Post Direct, avoided by diagonal TR up R wall of gully beyond a subsidiary ice pitch to gain snowfield. Climb directly until possible to regain main gully above big ice pitch. Remainder of gully is straightforward.

The Centre Post Direct (CP) grade IV

Photo E/46

Great ice pitch is climbed direct. This may be 150ft to 200ft high.

The North Pillar (6) grade IV 1500ft

Photo E/46

The buttress between the Centre and North Posts. Climb direct throughout. Only middle 500ft is inescapable and well defined from gullies each side. This section is at high angle and each pitch is more difficult than preceding.

The North Post (NP) grade IV 1500ft

Photo E/46

A hard frost and good plastering of snow and ice essential. The R-most and narrowest of the Posts. Open steep snow slopes lead to narrow chute with chockstone pitch. At point where gully widens, a vertical ice chimney in L-hand corner allows access to easy ledge leading to big platform on R. (An easy way up rocks on this side.) Recross final open face overlooking gully by 80ft TR (exposed). Then 100ft first R then back L leads to easy open couloir and top.

The Great Buttress (GB) grade IV 1000ft
Photo E/46
Start at lowest point on crag, R of North Post. Easy climbing for 250ft brings one to foot of Buttress proper. Starting approx 150ft R of North Post, follow Buttress up centre for five rope lengths, good B, but generally poor protection to Terrace. Climb steep Buttress above to top of face (crux), 150ft.

The South Pipe (7) grade III
Photo E/46, E/47, E/52
A fine alternative finish to gully – steep ice in narrow chimney. Less often in condition.

Staghorn Gully (8) grade III 1500ft
Photo E/46, E/47, E/52
On corner between the Post Face and the Inner Coire are two obvious parallel gashes on upper part of face, the North and South Pipes. Approach by shallow, half hidden gully called the Shelf, trending up R from base of North Post. (Normally steep snow.) Alternative approaches can be made up less obvious shelves on R. The North Pipe (easier of the two Pipes) is then followed – often a few short ice pitches. Directly above, gully opens to snow-basin just below plateau.

Direct Start (8a) grade III
Photo E/47, E/52
Take line of less obvious gully leading directly to Pipes. It usually provides several ice pitches.

Trespasser Buttress (T) grade IV 1000ft
Photo E/47, E/52, E/53)
This climb is between Staghorn Direct and Pumpkin. Start
near base of Staghorn Direct and gain chimney line on
buttress via steep start. Follow up chimney line until a bay is
reached (i.e. corner on L overhangs). Go R to gain short
chimney to reach overhanging bay. Continue R (long step R)
to gain the Diving Board. On up to gain top of rock step and
B. Follow chimney line and gain top of next step on L. Over
edge and up to crest. Follow up ridge to base of upper ridge
tier. Start this from chimney on R going L upwards TR to edge
of buttress and large detached blocks. Up these and continue
up edge to reach last step on buttress (Pumpkin exits from R).
Follow up chimney to R of ridge to top.

Pumpkin (9) grade IV 1000ft
Photo E/46, E/47, E/54
Climb obvious iced corner R of Trespasser Ridge. Ascend all
pitches direct. Upper chimney can be bypassed on L across
Trespasser Ridge and up easier snow slopes.

The Sash (S) grade II 800ft
Photo E/47
Often in condition. Start in narrow gully leading straight up
to huge parallel icefalls. Usually there is a certain amount of
ice. Under parallel icefalls, TR up L by series of snow ledges
towards plateau.

Diadem (D) grade II/III 700ft
Photo E/47, E/56
Start as for Sash, follow R parallel icefall. Bottleneck pitch at
bottom may require artificial ice technique if blocked by ice.
Easy snow above to base of long ice corner (150ft run out).
200ft of easy snow to exit.

The Wand, left branch of Diadem (L) grade III 250ft
Photo E/47, E/55
Climb very steep corner in four pitches to snow. Easier
climbing to plateau.

Cinderella (C) grade III 700ft
Photo E/47
The obvious gully in middle of Inner Coire face. Usually has
several short, easy-angled ice pitches, sometimes banked
over.

The Prow (P) grade II 700ft
Photo E/47
Leave Cinderella below halfway, trend steeply up side of
spur on R by ramp, and follow crest to cornice (usually large).

Crescent Gully (R) grade II 700ft
Photo E/47
This gully is situated in middle of cliffs beside the Window. R
wall is formidable and vertical. The start is a diminishing
snow ledge trending slightly L. Steep ice pitch then leads to
big upper amphitheatre (cornices usually avoidable).

Glencoe
Map: OS Tourist map, Ben Nevis and Glencoe, 1 in to 1 mile

Owing to easy access and its wide variety of winter climbing,
Glencoe is one of the most popular winter climbing regions
in Scotland. The north side of the Glen is bounded by the
wall of the Aonach Eagach Ridge, a superb excursion on a
good winter's day, yet technically not difficult for
experienced climbers.

The Buachaille: Approaching from the east the peak of
Stob Dearg rises above the expanse of Rannoch Moor. It is
known as the Buachaille to climbers; Stob Dearg forms the

NE summit of the massif and it is mainly upon this that the climbs are found. The north-west, north, east and south-east aspects of the mountain are uncompromisingly steep and descent should only be attempted down Coire na Tulaich. From the summit of Stob Dearg (3345ft, 1019m) go 300 yards along summit ridge SW (magnetic), then a descent of approx. 300 yards (cairns) takes you to the top of Coire na Tulaich (2900ft, 884m). You can also go south to Glen Etive from the top of Coire na Tulaich.

Opposite the Aonach Eagach Ridge, on the south side of the glen, is the Bidean nam Bian complex with its outriders Stob Coire nan Lochan, Stob Coire nam Beith, An t-Sron and the Three Sisters, Beinn Fhada, Gearr Aonach and Aonach Dubh. The photographs adequately show the various descent routes on these peaks. As Glencoe is owned by the National Trust for Scotland there is no restriction on camping and the Forestry Commission camp site is usually open in winter.

Buachaille

Crowberry Gully (Cg) grade III 1000ft
Photo E/57, E/58
This route is an excellent climb. In summer there are eight principal pitches with a fork near the top giving two finishes. During a heavy winter all pitches can be banked up but there can be up to five ice pitches. Crux usually is the TR R at junction of L and R forks. Above there is often at least one ice pitch and sometimes a P B on wall is necessary.

Left Fork (CL) grade IV
Photo E/58
This finish, usually done in two pitches, is hard and crux is last section up iced capstone (keep L at top). Finish up easy ice corridor to Crowberry Cap. Two rock P sometimes required.

North Buttress (N) grade III 1000ft
Photo E/57

This is the main buttress as seen in photograph of the Buachaille. It rises 1000ft from the base of the mountain to summit and, in winter, is a fine excursion. Best winter line is from bottom L where Buttress steepens in lower section, up chimney line towards the central chimney. From level with top of Raven's Gully the route is either up short chimney or to its L.

Agag's Groove (5) grade IV 350ft
Photo E/60

Climb up corner of wall beside rectangular block (just L of grooved arête). Up 90 ft to B at start of groove. Short corner a little below block B is crux. Follow groove 110 ft to B. Follow groove to easy L TR on open face beneath vertical nose. Up nose and L up to sloping top of block; 80ft. TR L and 75ft up face to ridge.

Route 1 (6) grade IV 230ft
Photo E/60, E/64

Up short chimney to L of rock rib, B; 40ft. Slant up R, take long slant up narrow shelf to ST, two sloping slabs, and above, a 15ft wall. Up wall, or TR L round corner, and up. Finish up long upper groove.

Raven's Gully (R) grade IV
Photo E/57, E/59, E/65

Raven's Gully gives an excellent winter climb of high standard. It is in condition during the winter more often than people realise, though pitch 4 (the crux) is seldom built up with snow. This was the crux in winter. The last pitch and indeed the second last can be formidable.

Alpen (1) grade IV 840ft
Photo E/60

Start at base of gully from a point half-way up the easy gully of Original Route of Central Buttress. Go up steep ledges to corner (150ft). Follow up corner to large cave (60ft). Ascend R wall of cave close to edge to upper chimney (30ft). Climb chimney, slant L to spike B (130ft). Go L to below the R side of two parallel chimneys (50ft). Climb this and ramp R to B (130ft). Climb open gully up L (140ft). Go up R on top of Buttress (150ft).

D Gully Buttress (2) grade III 800ft
Photo E/57, E/60
Approach as for Curved Ridge, but slant off L before steep section above Water Slab. D Gully is on its R (D Gully is grade II and, when filled in, gives no great difficulties). Reach the Buttress via the start of D Gully. Climb to steep slabby pitch. Though this can be turned on L it can be climbed direct (grade IV). Above the slab is the crux on the normal Buttress route, the Buttress narrows here. Higher it is possible to TR onto Curved Ridge and finish this route to below Crowberry Tower and then on to top.

Curved Ridge (3) grade II/III 1000ft
Photo E/57, E/60, E/63
Approach from above Water Slab on a TR to gain the base of Ridge. (To R is Easy Gully, between Curved Ridge and Rannoch Wall. This is usually grade I/II.) From the top of Curved Ridge you can TR up R behind Crowberry Tower (see photos E/58, E/63) or go directly up snow slope, top of D Gully, to where snow gains rocks, then go R up to summit.

North East Zig-Zag (7) grade III 600ft
Photo E/60
This is a mixture of various summer lines. The difficulties are mainly in the lower section which starts at the lower L of The Terrace, a broad ledge which runs round from Crowberry Gully.

North Face (N) grade IV 500ft

Photo E/60

A mixed route with difficulties on every pitch. Climb by a series of walls, corners and chimneys from a point R of NE edge of face. Climb a series of steep walls. Near the top is a short steep exposed crack. Beyond this it is easier to Heather Ledge, at extreme edge of SE face. Above is a large white scar on the north face. There is recess beneath it. Gain recess by TR round two pillars on the NE edge of Buttress. TR R beyond 10ft wall to short open corner. Climb chimney to gain platform. Now TR L to short steep crack near NE edge. Take edge to top.

Crowberrry Ridge, Direct by Abraham's Ledge (CR)
grade IV 750ft

Photo E/57, E/58, E/60

Start up steep crack from near start of Agag's Groove. Gain base of Ridge. Climb up to Abraham's Ledge. This is a small platform with a steep wall above. Move out L and up on balance holds. Difficult if iced. Slant slightly R and then directly up to Upper Ledge, 40ft above Abraham's (no runners). Above Upper Ledge TR L then up round corner. Now take easiest line to top. Upper section of route can be hard if verglassed. Finish over Crowberry Tower, or escape L at base of this to gain top of Curved Ridge. NB: It is also possible to avoid Abraham's Direct by going R a short way below on a TR line, then returning L again to join the normal route above Abraham's.

Garrick's Shelf (G) grade IV 650ft

Photo E/58

This shallow chimney line runs up parallel and L of Crowberry Gully on the R side of Crowberry Ridge. It often has a long continuous ice pitch in hard conditions. Start from Crowberry Gully; TR ledge of steeply shelving snow which gains first big pitch of Shelf. There is a cave here. There are three chimneys. The R wall and rib of middle chimney is usually the best way of gaining the Shelf ramp.

The route runs up the trough of the Shelf in several pitches and narrows and steepens and merges in the face above. This is beneath a small rectangular tower. Go R towards Crowberry Gully to square recess under pinnacle (often difficult at bulging corner). Beyond the pinnacle a broad groove hangs over the gully. Climb this, often icy, to gain crest of Crowberry Ridge. Either TR across to top of Curved Ridge, beneath Crowberry Tower, or climb Tower by edge near Crowberry Left Fork.

Great Gully (GG) grade I/II 1900ft
Photo E/57, E/59
Sometimes the lower gully can hold several ice pitches, and to the R and slightly higher than the start of Raven's a steep pitch can be awkward. It is also possible to TR into the gully from North Buttress, slightly below the level of the start of Raven's. (Subject to avalanches during and after heavy snowfall.)

The Chasm (C) grade III/IV 1500ft
Photo E/61, E/62
This gully starts a short way from the Glen Etive road, approx. one mile south by road from Coupall Bridge. If the gully is well filled up during an exceptionally severe winter it can be climbed without too much difficulty, but in the event of some of the pitches being iced, with lack of snow, it can become a hard and long route. Photo E/62 shows it reasonably well built up. There are possible variations higher up, with exits both L and R, but the direct route up the main watercourse usually gives the best and hardest line.

Long Rake (LR) grade I/II 1600ft
Photo E/61
This takes the approx. line of the Chasm to Crowberry Tower but it is possible to make harder variations from the ascending rake towards the summit (two of these are shown).

Otherwise the line can be continued to top of Curved Ridge.
V = variation finish.

Ladies' Gully (LG) grade IV 800ft
Photo E/61
This route is best done in a winter of heavy snowfall, with a good build-up. Start in gully which narrows higher presenting some difficulty before the ledge below the main ice pitch is gained. Climb the ice pitch by line of least resistance (this varies) 150ft to reach narrow chimney. Above it is easier back into gully bed. Beyond this an 80ft pitch (the summer crux) can present difficulties. Usually the groove L of overhanging section is used with a horizontal TR R at top. The last pitch before the fork gives a 30–40ft almost vertical ice pitch. Take either fork, they don't present any great difficulty.

Dalness Chasm, Right Fork (R) grade III 1200ft
Photo E/66
This gully is on the SE face of Stob na Broige and is obvious from the Glen Etive road, opposite Alltchaorunn (2½ miles up from Dalness House). It is seldom in condition and then usually immediately after heavy snowfall followed by frost. The R branch is the easiest. Reach junction of gully (J) by taking the true L side of gully to small chimney descending into R fork, a short way above J, abseil. Move up to ice pitch, climbed from R to L. Continue up, bearing R at further fork and climb to final narrowing section of gully, sometimes awkward.

Deirdre's Cleft (DC) grade II/III 800ft
Photo E/68, E/69, E/70
This climb starts from the ramp, across the River Etive on Beinn Ceitlein, just E of Dalness House, Glen Etive. Take the footbridge across river. The gully is obvious from the Glen Etive road. There are no particular difficulties in the lower section. Higher, either climb steep chimney direct or break out R up gully/scoop to exit just R of main gully line.

Sron na Lairig (2) grade II 1200ft

Photo E/71, E/72

This ridge is usually reached by the Glencoe road from the gorge or footpath starting opposite the big cairn at the signpost indicating the footpath to Glen Etive through the Lairig Eilde. No particular difficulties.

Glenmore Gully (5) grade II/III 500ft

Photo E/75

Ascend Chancellor Gully or true R edge to gain overhanging start of Glenmore Gully. Turn this up L then R. Up gully to large chockstone, climb wall to R and up into gully above. Finish up steep, partly enclosed scoop to top.

The Graduate (G) grade III/IV 500ft

Photo E/74

Take R corner of John Gray Buttress. Climb requires heavy snowfall followed by thaw and freeze-up.

John Gray Buttress (6) grade II 900ft

Photo E/75

Take a line close to Ingrid's Folly to steeper rock. Take easiest line up snow scoops with several TR. At definite chimney go up, then L, and slant R to steep step. Climb this direct. Continue up gully (tree B on R) and go R to gain edge of gully to top, or continue up gully line up steep pitch (crux) and on to top. Only suitable after heavy snowfall followed by frost.

Ingrid's Folly (7) grade II 900ft

Photo E/75

This route, together with the others on the lower part of this face, are sometimes suitable when the snow line is low and conditions are poor on the tops. Various pitches including a through route. In heavy soft/thaw snow, this route is subject to avalanche conditions.

Peregrine Gully (8) grade III 500ft

Photo E/75, E/76

Take Ingrid's Folly to above through-route, then TR up L into shallow gully line. There is one pitch before open snow slope leading to big chockstone. Turn this on L and follow up to under the great chockstone to top. It is also possible to finish last proper pitch of Ingrid's Folly (L TR pitch) and go horizontally L over mixed ground to gain Peregrine below great chockstone.

McArtney's Gully (9) grade III 500ft

Photo E/74, E/75, E/88

Approach from Ingrid's Folly (T, photo E/75) and Peregrine, or from lower reaches of Rev. Ted's Gully, or direct (see illustration). Ascend corner for several pitches to where gully steepens. Head for narrow rock chimney near centre and climb this and short groove above. Break out L either by ascending snowy ramp or L along TR to gain L corner.

Frostbite Wall (A) grade III/IV 680ft

Photo E/74, E/75

This route takes line of obvious icefall up main face between Rev. Ted's and McArtney Gullies.

Rev. Ted's Route (12) grade II/III 1000ft

Photo E/74, E/75, E/77, E/85

This gully is sometimes suitable when the snow line is low. The line of the gully is followed to the main fork. Direct route goes straight up in line with lower gully, but starts L up chimney, then out R then up, then L again. The R branch of the R fork (10) provides the easiest route and is generally easier than the lower gully. The chockstone finish, i.e. the L branch of the R fork (11), is the hardest and goes up direct under chockstones, P B. Flake B under second chockstone. Last pitch can be done straight up steep iced crack or L to easier ground, then up R.

Chancellor Gully (4) grade II/III 1700ft
Photo E/75
In icy conditions this gully can be quite hard, but such conditions are not frequent. It is best to enter gully from true L bank into junction. The gully can be finished by Glenmore Gully or continue on up.

Right Edge (a) grade III 300ft
Photo E/79
Take broad snowfield ramp on R face which runs up R under overhangs. The ramp is gained by chimney, below L side. From top of ramp take the arête to ridge.

Sabre Tooth (c) grade III 400ft
Photo E/79, E/80
Go up right into snow bay, B in corner. Go out R to edge then up to terrace (easy route off L along ledge). Go L along terrace to steep corner, B. Up corner then R along ledge to B. Follow chimney/grooves to top.

Pterodactyl (d) grade IV 350ft
Photo E/79
Go directly up to obvious overhanging entry, which forms the bottom of steep chimney line on upper section of buttress. The entry into the upper chimney is the crux.

Tyrannosaur (5) grade IV 400ft
Photo E/79
This climb takes the well-defined R edge of the L section of cliff, starting on R wall well below corner of Pterodactyl and some 30ft up from lowest rocks. Start up short shallow chimney and follow thin crack continuation which trends slightly L and over buttress edge to reach snow bay. From snow bay a steep corner crack is followed up to L of crest. Final section of climb gives two long pitches of easier climbing by steep snow grooves close to crest.

Dislocation (7) grade III 280ft
Photo E/79

This climb is on R-hand side wall of buttress and leaves the
gully about 50ft above the toe of the buttress. A groove line
which trends slightly R is followed to snowpatch, above which
a shallow broken chimney leads to top.

Trilobite (8) grade II/III 200ft
Photo E/79

Go up steep groove from a point where Right-Hand Gully
(photo E/78) starts to narrow. Climb to top trending L on
upper part.

Lost Valley: Gearr Aonach, far East Face
Gully A, Right Fork (A) grade IV 800ft
Photo E/83, E/85

Reach gully proper up steep initial pitch, either direct or on
the L. The route above, where the gully steepens, is obvious,
keeping to the R up steep ice scoop then up ice bulge in
chimney, P B above. Follow on up true gully bed to top.

Lost Leeper (LL) grade III 600ft
Photo E/85

This is next definite snow/ice chimney line to R of Gully A and
skirting L edge of E face of Gearr Aonach. Take line of
approach (in winter) as shown in photograph and ascend
narrow ice chimney to L of main face. After a rope length
break out L to gain further ice chimney and ascend this and
continuation to bay below steep ice pitch (small tree B). Climb
ice pitch direct and remaining pitch to top. Mainly P B
throughout.

Mome Rath (M) grade IV 310ft
Photo E/82, E/85

Climb by ledges and ramps to ledge at foot of steep exposed
chimney. Ascend this till it fades out at approx. 60ft. Make a
L TR into another chimney. Climb this for a short way to a bay

on L. Climb a slabby ice-plated rib on L leading to short corner chimney (steep) at top of cliff.

The Wabe (W) grade IV 300ft

Photo E/81, E/85

This route follows icefall more or less in line with the summer route, starting about 75ft R of Mome Rath. Up 20ft to snow ledge, then up rock and ice trending L to small ST and flake B, 10ft below prominent nose, 150ft. Pass nose on L then up R and L to B on block, 70ft. Follow up recessed section to ST on rib, 50ft. Go R and up, then L on to top, 150ft.

Beinn Fhada, West Face

The Midge (1) grade II/III 400ft

Photo E/84

Follow crest of buttress starting to L of Wasp. It is possible to finish via gully from wide snow ledge.

The Wasp (2) grade III 400ft

Photo E/84

This climb is on the buttress to L of main summit, see photograph. Ascend a narrow twisting chimney for 2 pitches with hard moves at top of each pitch. Continue easily to top of buttress.

The Cleg (3) grade III 400ft

Photo E/84

This climb is to R of Wasp and follows a diagonal line running from near start of Wasp on rock wall. Crux is narrow hanging scoop. Continue up buttress to summit.

Broken Lip Gully (4) grade II 580ft

Photo E/84

Follow chimney/gully line from L side of buttress, from snow bay to top. It runs just parallel to Main Buttress.

Beinn Fhada, NW Face

Main Buttress (5) grade II 700ft
Photo E/84

Take a direct line up buttress, going slightly R after first pitch to ascend short snow gully. Break L to buttress, various lines to top.

Twine Climb (6) grade II 600ft
Photo E/84

Go up chimney scoop line and TR L along snow to take parallel line to Main Buttress to top.

Quintet (7) grade III 440ft
Photo E/84

This climb follows the snowy corridor which cuts diagonally across the face from L to R. Start from ramp going directly up iced chimney to block B; 70ft. Continue up to narrowing section of gully and bridge up and R over edge to gain the true corridor. An awkward section 70ft above leads to easier ground; continue up corridor to near top of buttress.

The Ramp (8) grade II 700ft
Photo E/84

Follow line up ramp, then to crest, then up summit.

Further West Face, Gearr Aonach (approach by Coire nan Lochan valley)

Farewell Gully (F) grade III 500ft
Photo E/86

This gully is obvious from the high path to Stob Coire nan Lochan. There are a number of steep short pitches. Route can be hard if there is a poor build-up of ice.

Ciotach Route (1) grade II/III 300ft
Photo E/86
Go L from 999 approach and gain icy section rising to ridge.
Variation possible.

Rescue Team Gully (2) grade III 250ft
Photo E/86
This is the very steep short gully directly ahead as you
approach. Ascend iced chimney.

Jim's Gully (3) grade III 320ft
Photo E/86
This starts as for 999 or more direct up from L of start of this
route. Following curving line of gully to top.

999 (4) grade III 400ft
Photo E/86, E/87
This is the R of the three gullies. Take R fork at junction and
ascend to where R gully (Jim's Gully) goes up steeply towards
tree. Climb this and finish either in true continuation or
ascend narrow chimney going up L. This route has many
caves and chimneys and finishes in steep chockstone capped
corner. Break out R at top. 5 = easier variation finish of 999.

Stob Coire nan Lochan

Easy Face Route (14) grade I 850ft
Photo E/78, E/88
Straightforward climb.

Boomerang Gully (3) grade II 850ft
Photo E/88
Take easy snow slope into gully to pitch on R. This leads into
gully above, often iced. It is easier to go straight on and reach
top up face, or by 2, the left branch, grade II.

Scabbard Chimney (Sc) grade IV 500ft
Photo E/89

This route is seldom in good winter condition. Climb from close to lowest rocks of Summit Buttress up obvious chimney slanting up R. The crux, a sentry box, 200ft up, may need direct aid. A gully on the L above chimney leads to arête.

Spectre (G) grade IV 400ft
Photo E/89

This route runs parallel to Scabbard Chimney, and starts 40ft to R of that route. Up wall, 70ft to a point under first main chimney section of Scabbard Chimney. Go up R to gain snow ledge, follow this for 20ft and down 8ft to long shelf. Up ice bulge above and groove to P B. Climb slab above, 25ft to bulge, continue 70ft to wide ledge. TR into the gully finish of Scabbard Chimney.

Innuendo (I) grade IV 500ft
Photo E/89

Start level with bottom of Dorsal Arête. It takes an obvious chimney-groove for 120ft to ledge on L then goes on up into an overhung bay. Exit is by crack on R wall (crux) and easy snow is followed diagonally R to a block B below upper wall. TR R beneath a hanging chimney until steep cracks lead back L into chimney above overhang. The chimney is climbed direct, and easier slope to edge of Boomerang Gully.

Langsam (L) grade II 700ft
Photo E/89

This route starts from Broad Gully and goes up snow slope to under rock wall. There are two routes from this point. First route: TR L on steep snow up then R to enter short gully and so to top bearing slightly R to summit. Alternatively take chimney under wall from top of first pitch under rock wall and climb this top. Continue TR under wall and ascend steeper snow up L (crux), to gain easy snow line to summit.

Pearly Gates (not marked) grade II 500ft
Photo E/89
This route leaves Broad Gully half way up on L (just under
the figure 5) and a narrow gap is visible on the skyline. Go up
in zigzags to this point, 150ft, and go through gap and follow
to top via Langsam line.

Broad Gully (4) grade I 600ft
Photo E/88, E/89
(Access route)

Dorsal Arête (5) grade II 300ft
Photo E/88, E/89, E/92
A rock arête situated between Broad and Forked Gullies.
Access from Broad Gully at base of arête. At top finish by
slab to R or by chimney (steep) on L (above narrow arête).
Variation starts.

Forked Gully, Right Fork **(F)** grade II
               Left Fork **(F)** grade I 500ft
Photo E/88, E/89
The L fork gives an easy snow climb. The R (R of 200ft rock
rib) is steeper and holds ice.

Twisting Gully (T) grade II/III 500ft
Photo E/88, E/89
This gully is separated from Forked Gully by an indefinite
rib; to its R is South Buttress. The route takes the line of a
shallow gully. Go up 100ft into recess. From this point there
are two continuations. The original route takes chimney on L
to bulge, then TR L across gully wall to reach L rib.
Mantelshelf move on short arête, then easier above to final
snow fan.

Right Fork (T) grade III
Photo E/88, E/89

This is a more difficult and direct line on the middle section of original route. From recess, take steep ice pitch up corner. A broken rib separates this from original route. The original route is gained under final fan.

South Buttress (S) grade IV 500ft
Photo E/89

At centre of buttress, 100ft up, there is an obvious undercut rock nose. L is deep chimney, the base of which comes down to 50ft above narrow ledge, which runs round Buttress. Start below this chimney and keep L to gain large ledge beneath wall. TR L across top of deep groove to start of wide ledge (this runs horizontally into Twisting Gully). At other end a chimney cuts this. Climb chimney to top and follow straight up until possible to TR L into gully leading to top. Various lines possible in upper section.

SC Gully (SC) grade III 500ft
Photo E/88, E/89

This is the steep gully between Central and South Buttresses. There is usually an ice pitch low down, which can be turned on L. Go up on steep snow to point where R TR is made to gain a gangway (sometimes with bulge before top). P B often necessary. Steep and straightforward climbing to top.

Central Buttress (10) grade III 550ft
Photo E/88, E/89

From a bay go up to R to gain crest. Up ridge to tower (turn on R) and regain crest by short chimney. Continue to top.

NC Gully (NC) grade I/II 600ft
Photo E/89

The gully is between steep flanking walls. There can be an ice pitch short way up with B in cave on R.

Evening Citizen (C) grade IV 300ft
Photo E/89, E/91
This takes the corner line R of NC Gully. Climb
corner/chimney and up steeply onto crest.

North Face (11) grade III 300ft
Photo E/88, E/89
From under steep rock at bottom of North Buttress TR R to
snow ledge. Ascend to recess high up on face. Up steep
groove from L end of ledge to a nose and an arête.

North Gully (N) grade I/II 250ft
Photo E/88, E/89, E/90
This gully separates North Buttress from Pinnacle Buttress.
Only the last section of gully is steep. Climb ice groove
leading to R of cornice and turn the latter usually on R or
tunnel (sometimes very large cornice). Exit just R of North
Gully.

Right Chimney (not marked) grade II 250ft
Photo E/88
Climb obvious ice chimney to R of North Gully, last pitch
crux, climb up crack to L or easier to R.

Pinnacle Gully (13) grade I 200ft
Photo E/88
The easy R-hand gully of the corrie.

Aonach Dubh, North Face

Findlay's Rise (F) grade III 500ft
Photo E/93, E/96
This is an obvious icefall on the L of face which usually forms
by mid-winter if there has been sufficient frost. Climb ice
direct and continue up buttress, which can be awkward.

Ossian's Close (not marked) grade III 500ft

Photo E/94

This is the obvious deep gully to L of Ossian's Cave. The difficulties are in the lower part, the upper being an easy slope. Climb up initial steep pitch just above the traverse path immediately below cliff. Gain enclosed gully and move up to large chockstone pitch. Climb this on the L wall and B in cave. Climb steeply out of cave to B in upper easy gully. The climb can be finished by taking the buttress on the L which gives a grade II termination to the climb.

Late Night Special (L) grade III 700ft

Photo E/93

This is the snow scoop L of Shadbolt's Chimney. There are two separate starts, both up steep ice. Above the route slants L and is thereafter easier. Alternatively finish as for Shadbolt's.

Shadbolt's Chimney (S) grade IV 700ft

Photo E/93

This climb is to L of Ossian's Cave. Go up deep chimney from the Sloping Shelf for 150ft. Up buttress on R, or up to 30ft chimney which leads to the amphitheatre. A wide snow gully leads to top. This route is seldom in true winter conditions.

Pleasant Terrace (P) grade II/III 800ft

Photo E/93

Start from the upper R end of Sloping Shelf. Climb from bay L of Deep Gash Gully. Go up L in two pitches. The second can be hard and starts as a corner crack. The Terrace narrows to a spectacular ledge going horizontally L for several hundred ft. The ledge broadens after a slight descent, under a deep narrow chimney; this is taken to the top, F, or finish by Shadbolt's.

Deep Gash Gully (DG) grade IV 200ft

Photo E/93

This is the obvious gully just above end of the Shelf. Though the climb is short it is technically hard. There is a 30ft chimney pitch, a steep ice pitch leading to the main overhang. A thread B in a hole in the roof is used and up rope using slings to gain B. The final pitch, 40ft, entails going through a small hole feet first. An ice overhang is climbed above. Steep snow to top.

Bidean nam Bian

North Route (1) grade II/III 700ft

Photo E/97

This route takes the L edge of the buttress by scoops and chimneys to rock arête. (Escape to L possible.)

North Route Variation (2) grade III 220ft

Photo E/97

This climb takes an obvious scoop to R of North Route. The scoop is steep and finally overhangs. Climb arête to the R and make short horizontal TR round corner into further scoop. Snow-covered slabs and crack (crux) lead to ledge above the overhang of initial scoop. TR L to crest of North Route.

Central Gully (CG) grade I 450ft

Photo E/97, E/98, E/100

This gully is between Church Door and Diamond Buttresses. The bottom of the gully is divided by Collie's Pinnacle. The main branch (R) is straightforward and continues directly to top. There is a further branch to the L near top and yet another to the R. The top R is harder. The bottom fork to L of Collie's Pinnacle (L) can be difficult.

West Chimney (C) grade IV 700ft

Photo E/97, E/101, E/102

Ascend L slanting chimney to under, then up, large

chockstones to B under overhang; 150ft. Up short steep wall
to gain cave and through-route to roof. Go R from exit
chimney to Flake Route Arch and B. Continue across gap to B
under steep crack above Crypt Route (exposed). Up crack, B
at top. Follow up, slanting L, then up icy slab to summit
slopes. The section from Flake Route up is also used for
Crypt Route.

Crypt Route (Ct) grade III/IV 180ft
Photo E/98, E/101, E/102

Go up chimney, 70ft to rock passage which goes into buttress.
From back of passage (dark) are various routes: *Tunnel Route*:
through narrow passage in L wall, into rock chamber (total
darkness). A further tunnel goes to second chamber; from
this a long narrow tunnel goes up to aperture in face of cliff,
20ft below R side of arch. Up 20ft to hole in lower R end of
arch. Continue by ordinary Flake Route. *Through Route*:
ascend cave-like end of passage to second smaller cave. Direct
exit is overhanging and spectacular.

Gallery Variation: (Ct) grade III/IV 180ft
Photo E/98, E/101, E/102

Take through route to second cave, ascend into another
chimney in same fault going to third cave (smaller). Go into
the Gallery above, 6 × 20 × 4ft high. Go down 4ft from
Gallery floor and, facing downwards, TR 50ft R and climb up
to base of arch. Routes finish as West Chimney.

Flake Route (Ct) grade IV 350ft
Photo E/98, E/101, E/102

Up crack to top of Buttress, above flake, make awkward step
R round corner. Straight up until L TR can be done to arch of
Church Door. Cross arch to a 30ft chimney (crux). Face R
wall. Above chimney up steep face to easy ground under
cairn, or avoid face by harder chimney on its L. Finish as
West Chimney.

Hourglass Gully (A) grade I 400ft

Photo E/99

This gully is straightforward, but sometimes has two short pitches.

The Gash (C) grade III/IV 400ft

Photo E/99

Reach gully by rising TR L from bottom of Hourglass Gully, or ascend direct, ST on R. Direct up steep ice and bulges above. Climb overhanging chockstone on L to cave under second big chockstone slab. Up through-route at back of cave to narrow exit.

The Hash (2) grade II/III 400ft

Photo E/99

Start just R of Gash and follow shallow chimney line to top.

Stob Coire nam Beith

Broken Gully (1, 2) grade II 500ft

Photo E/104

Ascend L into recess above wide snow shelf which cuts Buttress 1 into two tiers. 100ft up, a shallow gully on R is taken to easy L TR to top of buttress. The L fork is harder and holds more ice.

Buttress 1 (3) grade II/III 700ft

Photo E/104

Up chimney line in a series of ice pitches. Above chimney TR easily L to reach top of buttress, or continue to summit.

Arch Gully (4) grade II/III 600ft

Photo E/104

This Gully is between Buttresses 1 and 2. The lower section is usually banked over, but can give a few pitches. A narrowing slope leads to two steep ice pitches, which can be climbed direct, or turned without much trouble. Easy slopes to top (400ft).

Central Gully (5) grade III/IV 1500ft

Photo E/104

This gully starts above and just L of the lowest rocks of
Buttress 3. It holds a lot of ice.

Deep Cut Chimney (DC) grade III/IV 1500ft

Photo E/104

This climb offers several short ice pitches, the longest usually
40ft. After approx. 400ft the Chimney reaches a small
amphitheatre where it is easy to continue to the R to crest of
Buttress 4, close to fork of North West Gully. From the
amphitheatre, the L fork can be hard if covered with verglas.
This line goes L taking long steep crack line to easier ground
above.

North West Gully (6) grade III 1500ft

Photo E/104

Variation possible on this route: start as shown on illustration
or TR in from R from bottom of the Pyramid. Easy up to L of
Sphinx Buttress; above gully has two forks. The L one is
straightforward. The R fork goes up L of upper section of the
Sphinx, several hundred feet to further fork. The L fork can
have an ice pitch leading to shoulder (steep wall to L of
shoulder can be quite hard sometimes). Easy to top from
shoulder.

Smashed Spectacles Gully (7) grade II/III 500ft

Photo E/104

This is the R of two diverging couloirs. There is a short ice
pitch in first part, followed by a very steep chimney with ice
bulge above. Above, easier to top.

Adagio (L) grade IV 500ft

Photo E/103, E/105, E/106

This climb is on W side of buttress to R of Summit Gully. It
takes line of a steep narrow gully. Easy snow leads to a
steeper section with thinly iced wall on L. This is passed by
climbing a corner on R and making a difficult L-rising TR

round corner to gain other ice chimney. This L chimney is climbed for 20ft before moving into R-hand one above bulge. Go up R chimney 50ft. This leads to easier ground. The continuation follows main gully (keeping L) to big cave which is climbed direct. Gully now leads out on to top of buttress. Continue easily by ridge of Summit Gully or use Summit Gully as descent route. NB: Belays inadequate.

Hidden Gully (HG) grade III 500ft
Photo E/105
Climb to cave and up on L wall. Easy to further cave, passed on L by short ice pitch. Ahead is a saddle above a rib in centre of gully. The gully narrows and steepens above and a short chimney is climbed. There are two narrow exits above; take the L. It is steeper at top. Finish up Adagio or go R to Bootneck Gully.

Bootneck Gully B grade II/III 800ft
Photo E/105
This route takes a central line up W face of Stob Coire nam Beith. It takes central chimney line which has a steep rock wall on its R with a possibly easier gangway start close under this. (The next chimney L leads to the top of a small rock buttress and goes up near Hidden Gully.) After two pitches in gully/chimney a steep ice wall on R is climbed direct (crux). This leads on to long easy snow slopes which lead to summit of mountain, bearing R at fork.

The Chasm of An t-Sron grade II/III 1200ft
(no illustration)
This chasm splits the north face and starts at about 1000ft, clearly visible from the road. Five pitches; but most of the gully is easy. Three of the pitches are waterfalls and can give good ice pitches. The first, a large one, is avoided on the L flank. Seldom in true winter conditions.

Aonach Dubh, West Face

Dinner-Time Buttress (d) grade I 600ft
Photo E/107

This buttress provides a means of access to Stob Coire nan Lochan. The usual route is to turn into Gully 2 at the start of the upper rock and ascend gully. The Buttress itself can provide a pleasant climb in icy conditions. The TR to Middle Ledge can be awkward in winter and a difficult sloping shelf is followed (frequently iced) up and round corner to R from the start of the easy upper section of Gully 2. Another approach is via lower section of B Buttress. Gully 1 is of little interest and is rather indefinite. Gully 2 offers a good descent route, though steep, and shouldn't be glissaded.

B Buttress, the Pinnacle Face (B) grade III 300ft
Photo E/107

Climb up B Buttress to Middle Ledge. From just below Middle Ledge, three pinnacles can be seen above. To the L of pinnacles a groove runs down. Up a chimney, under L pinnacle and R of groove towards R pinnacle.

Cyclop (Cy) grade III/IV 350ft
Photo E/107

At start of Middle Ledge a steep corner goes directly up buttress. Climb this direct. Take chimney line above to gain the 'eye' of the buttress. Through eye then up buttress direct to top.

Gully 3 (3) grade II/III 1000ft
Photo E/107

The gully is shallow and somewhat indefinite. It is better defined where it cuts the Middle Tier.

C Buttress (C) grade II 500ft
Photo E/107

Go across from Middle Ledge or up lower part of B Buttress.

Climb up a short wide chimney on the R and take the obvious crest.

The Screen (S) grade III 200ft
Photo E/107, E/108
This is the prominent icefall which forms on the lower tier to R of Gully 3. It gives a direct start to C-D Scoop which is between C and D Buttresses on Middle Tier. By TR R ascend 70ft to icicle recess, TR R and back L above to final ice runnel.

C-D Scoop (K) grade II 500ft
Photo E/107
This route can be reached from Gully 2 and is the second gully on L. The route gives two short pitches. Exit along The Rake, or continue by the hidden branch of a gully to L, the continuation of Gully 3 above The Rake. The route makes a good continuation to The Screen.

D Buttress (D) grade II 500ft
Photo E/107
Up steep prominent icy gangway just R of C-D Scoop. Above, go R, L and R on zigzagging ramps and ledges, to crest and take short steep grooved wall. Easier above.

Amphitheatre Scoop, Direct (A) grade IV 1000ft
Photo E/107
Start below Middle Ledge at line of steep ice leading up to Middle Ledge. Climb this and from the Ledge follow up for 150ft on steep ice column in rear of corner. Beyond the angle eases in the upper gully to The Rake; an easy finish goes up snow ramp to top, or TR L back along The Rake to No. 2 Gully.

The Slot (V) grade II 300ft
Photo E/107, E/110
Start from The Rake above E Buttress and follow the slope R of and below Amphitheatre North Ridge. This becomes a

shallow gully with an awkward cave pitch above, exiting to a deep crevasse.

Amphitheatre North Ridge (V) grade III 300ft
Photo E/107
This ridge gives a good finish above The Rake for the routes on the Middle Tier. It can be used as a finish for The Slot and Amphitheatre Scoop. It starts above and slightly R of the easy upper gully of Amphitheatre Scoop. A series of small cracks and grooves leads up front of steep step to crest.

Gully 4 (4) grade III/IV 1200ft
Photo E/107, E/109
This gully gives several ice pitches (climbers encircled above the 4 in photo E/109). The lower pitches can be avoided by TR Middle Ledge. Follow up under side wall of E Buttress then slant L. A ramp leading up L here joins The Rake and opposite, escape is possible along Rake continuation to Coire Beith. However, Gully 4 now narrows to deep cleft following L to gain summit slopes. Near top, on R a narrow snow chimney is grade III and provides a harder finish. The deep crevasse of The Slot is high on the L wall of the gully (where it narrows) but is not gained from Gully 4.

Christmas Eaves (CE) grade III/IV 300ft
Photo E/109
This is a variation to Christmas Couloir. Take a central line when opposite the base of the ramp leading to The Rake and climb it into corner. Move up R and regain Christmas Couloir above on main snow slope.

Christmas Couloir (CC) grade III 800ft
Photo E/107, E/109
Start from Middle Ledge or Gully 4 and follow up keeping R of main gully. The crux is above the TR line connecting The Rake across Gully 4. It usually gives steep ice. Above the route goes up recess in upper cliff. There are three finishes, direct is hardest.

Camel, F Buttress (Ca) grade III/IV 900ft

Photo E/107

This starts to L of variant start to No. 5 Gully. Take easiest line to Middle Ledge continuation. The lower section is seldom in condition. From Middle Ledge follow up via the Needle's Eye, which is the deep rock chimney just L of upper part of No. 5 Gully.

Gully 5, Left Start (5) grade IV 1000ft

Photo E/107

To avoid lower overhanging ice pitch, Elliot's Downfall, start further L at subsidiary gully. Climb chimney to small cave. Move up and R over ice fall to reach crest of small buttress. Climb buttress to below Needle's Eye (approx. line of original route). Move R into gully proper and continue up gully over one small ice pitch at the bottom, taking L fork at point where gully is split by rib at above half height.

Elliot's Downfall (i) grade V/VI 200ft

Photo E/107, E/111

This is the icicle which usually descends and connects in cold conditions at the base of Gully 5. It is a hard technical problem and subject to certain danger during thaw.

Gully 6 (6) grade III/IV 800ft

Photo E/107, E/112

This gully usually gives a continuous ice climb in good conditions. Several fine pitches.

Chaos Chimney (Ch) grade III 500ft

Photo E/107

This is the chimney/gully R of Gully 6. Start at base of chimney at bottom of 6 and climb two small ice pitches to where chimney deepens and narrows. Up large ice pitch on L and then on R. Continue over two further ice pitches to top.

Sgor na h-Ulaidh

Access to this peak is up a side road opposite Achnacon Farm at the W end of Glencoe. Walk up this road, round farm and keep to the L fork of the Allt na Muide to Sgor na h-Ulaidh ahead and to the L. Vixen Gully can be used for descent when there is sufficient snow to blank out the small pitches, or the descent as shown on the photograph leading on to the easy ridge of Aonach Dubh a'Chinne (R).

Subsidiary Scoop (1) grade II 500ft
Photo E/115
Just L of Red Gully on other side of rocky rib a line up steep snow is taken with short ice steps.

Red Gully (2) grade III 650ft
Photo E/115
Climb gully direct which often has considerable ice late in the season. Some years the gully can be harder.

Brush Buttress (3) grade III 900ft
Photo E/115
This buttress is in three tiers, the middle one being the hardest. Start from lowest rocks and climb direct. Start main buttress in central gully and move to edge on L. Gain ledge and B above; 80ft. Start in chimney above and climb this and B on L; 60ft. Continue up chimney line and TR R of narrow ledge. Finish on final buttress to L of steep edge, or up last section of main gully.

Vixen Gully (4) grade I 500ft
Photo E/115
An easy route to the summit, can sometimes be used for descent.

West Gully (5) grade I 1000ft
Photo E/115
A straight snow climb, sometimes a bit awkward at top.

Aonach Eagach

Red Funnel Gully (R) grade II/III 700ft
Photo E/120, E/121
This route is easily reached from main road by the big cairn (see illustration). It is suitable when there has been a heavy snowfall and higher routes are out of condition. The gully cuts the face of A'Chailleach and L branch should be taken. A 40ft pitch bars the way where R wall overhangs. Climb this and follow up main gully. It gets narrower nearer top. Return via summit, or TR on R into coire to E of peak and descend.
NB: As the gully starts low down, frost is necessary for a good climb.

Aonach Eagach Ridge (not marked) grade I/II 3 miles
Photo E/75, E/112, E/120, E/122, E/123, E/124, E/125
The Ridge is usually traversed from E to W starting at lay-by near Meeting of Three Waters. Start up true R of Allt-an-Ruigh and cross this some 200 yards uphill and continue up side of stream, or take ridge to top of Am Bodach without crossing stream. The steep descent from Am Bodach can be one of the most difficult sections. On no account descend from the Ridge until the TR has been completed as a great number of accidents has occurred to parties doing so. Descent should only be down easy slopes leading to Loch Achtriochtan (see photo) or from the col between Sgor nam Fiannaidh and the Pap of Glencoe. In deep soft snow conditions the former route can avalanche. The path which follows the true R of Clachaig Gully, though a good ascent route, can be difficult to locate from above.
NB: Wind and snow conditions should be taken into account on this route.

Clachaig Gully (not marked) grade IV 1735ft
Photo E/113
This climb is one of the most popular summer climbs in

Glencoe (it starts just above Clachaig Hotel). The climb is obvious as far as Great Cave Pitch, where the route goes right to a small tree growing from a crack on the rock face. From the tree a downwards, then horizontal TR leads to top of pitch. The short pitch following is probably crux of climb and above this, after short chockstone pitch, is Jericho Wall. This 70ft wall is to R of waterfall. There are several other good pitches above, the Red Chimney being the most significant. The best route for descent is by the W bank. There is a good escape route below the Great Cave Pitch up the W wall, through the small trees.

Farm Gully (1) grade III 800ft
Photo E/75, E/123, E/124

This is the obvious R branch of the wide gully, which runs up to crest of ridge. Start of gully is awkward, and the bottom few pitches, unless there is an usually heavy snowfall, are best avoided up steep snow slope on L with some tree B. Several ice pitches. If this route is done during sunshine there can be a danger of falling stones.

Twenty Minute Gully (2) grade III 600ft
Photo E/75, E/123, E/124

This is first obvious narrow gully down from crest of Ridge below steep step to W of Am Bodach. Gully curves L and provides an excellent means of gaining summit when TR Ridge from W to E.

Vice Chancellor Ridge (V) grade II/III 700ft
Photo E/123, E/124, E/126

This is obvious ridge just L of Big Chock Gully. Ascend directly up ridge from snow slope to first rocky tower. Continue in two rope lengths to more formidable tower, take central line. Above, a rocky wall is climbed to gain top of further more exposed tower. TR narrow snow arête at rear to easier ground. Reach a steep step in ridge in a further rope length. This can be climbed direct (slightly to R of centre), severe, or take easy gully on R to reach easy ground leading to summit.

Big Chock Gully (BC) grade III 700ft
Photo E/123, E/124
This route is the obvious gully to L of Chancellor Buttress. The main difficulty is surmounting the big chockstone pitch halfway up. This is climbed on R wall on ice; seldom in condition and requires a very big build-up of snow and ice.

The Chancellor (3) grade III/IV 1000ft
Photo E/75, E/123, E/124
There are two starts to this route, a shallow snow gully which runs up into buttress or the ridge to R. There can be difficulty route-finding on this climb, especially in steeper middle section where it is better to keep L.

Old Man Gully (om) grade II 900ft
Photo E/123, E/124
This prominent gully gives a good climb to summit of Am Bodach in heavy, hard snow conditions. The gully can be entered from L and some of the lower pitches can be by-passed. Various exits at top, which can be sometimes steep and corniced. Access to gully base is up scree/snow slope from main road directly below col to W of Am Bodach, towards low point on ridge. Keep to true R of small stream on approach.

Stob a'Ghlais Choire (3207ft, 977m)
Photo E/127
Access to this peak is from Black Rock Cottage on the ski tow road at the E end of Glencoe. Slant across moor round ridge of Creag Dhubh (small cliffs on L) and gain main basin of peak. Routes 1, 2 and 3 are all easy pleasant gully lines suitable for winter. Descend by first main coire on L on S of summit or traverse round ridge to Meall a'Bhuiridh (3636ft) and descend alongside ski tows. A = Access route, D = a

descent route. The long buttress to the right of 3 also gives a pleasant winter route; take easiest line.

Stob Ghabhar (3565 ft, 1087m)
Map: OS Tourist Map, Ben Nevis and Glencoe, 1 in to 1 mile, OS No. 50, Glen Orchy, 1:50,000
Photo E/128
.This is the peak to the S of Rannoch Moor. Access via Forest Lodge (west end of Loch Tulla). The Central Couloir (CC., grade I) faces the NE and holds snow well.

Coire an Dothaidh, Bridge of Orchy
Map: No. 50, Glen Orchy, 1:50,000
Photo E/129
This is the corrie due E of Bridge of Orchy. Go up from station and follow stream. Route 1 gives a grade II climb and Route 2 a grade III when the ice is formed.

Ben Lui, Tyndrum (3708ft, 1130m)
Map: OS No. 50, Glen Orchy, 1:50,000
Photo E/130, E/131
This peak, though not offering much in the way of climbing, can provide a pleasant day to or from the more serious mountains to the west and north. Climbs 1, 2 and 3 are all about grade I and approach is from either Tyndrum Station (Lower) via the forestry road, or from the A82 and bridge over the River Fillan.

Captions to illustrations
E/1   Ben Nevis left with the Carn Mor Dearg Arête in front of the east face of North-East Buttress. *H. MacInnes*

E/2   Ben Nevis from lower Steall, Glen Nevis. BN = Ben Nevis: a = start of abseil posts, A = Carn Mor Dearg, SG = Steall Gully, a grade I/II climb. The dotted line indicates one route of ascent from the Waterslide, just short of the terminal car park, Glen Nevis. *H. MacInnes*

E/3   Carn Mor Dearg Arête. The abseil posts start from the horizontal part of the Arête on right. This photograph was taken mid-May. *H. MacInnes*

E/4   The 'Little Brenva', the east face of North East Buttress (NEB). OR = Observatory Ridge. FP = First Platform. d = abseil posts. GT = Great Tower, Tower Ridge. Carn Mor Dearg Arête on left. *H. MacInnes*

E/5   Upper section, Route Major, Carn Mor Dearg Arête below left. *H. MacInnes*

E/6   The North East Buttress with Carn Mor Dearg Arête (CA) on left. fp = First Platform. Or = Observatory Ridge. Ob = Observatory Buttress. *H. MacInnes*

E/7   Minus Three Gully. *S. Grymble*

E/8   Minus Two Gully, fourth pitch. *A. Kimber*

E/9   Astronomy, with Zero Gully behind climber. *H. MacInnes*

E/10   Looking down Astronomy with Zero Gully running up diagonally left and with two climbers on East Face, Observatory Ridge. *A. Fyffe*

E/11   The Orion Direct, note solo climber slightly above half-way up photograph. Photograph taken from Observatory Ridge. *P. Moores*

E/12   Orion Direct, Upper Basin. C = CIC Hut. *A. Kimber*

E/13   First pitch, Zero Gully. *A. Kimber*

E/14   Higher up Zero Gully. *P. Moores*

E/15   Looking across Orion Face to Tower Bridge. Et = Eastern Traverse. Arrows indicate climbers. Lower arrow shows climber on Slav Route. *N. Keir*

E/16   The finish of Tower Ridge. Great Tower below climber. *H. MacInnes*

E/17   North East Buttress and Tower Ridge, Ben Nevis. CA = Carn Mor Dearg Arête. d = abseil posts. fp = First Platform. z = Zero Gully. DB = Douglas Boulder. Cg = Comb Gully. Cb = Comb Buttress. tg = Tower Gully. Gg = Gardyloo Gully. *H. MacInnes*

E/18   Tower Ridge with Observatory Buttress on left

above start of Observatory Ridge (OR). Gg = Gardyloo Gully, Tg = Tower Gully, Et = Eastern Traverse, g = Garadh Gully, DB = Douglas Boulder, Ta = Approach for Tower Ridge. *H. MacInnes*

E/19   An aerial view of Tower Ridge. V = Vanishing Gully, I = Italian Climb, g = Garadh Gully. *H. MacInnes*

E/20   Hadrian's Wall and Point Five Gully. *M. Ross*

E/21   Climbers in Point Five Gully. *M. Ross*

E/22   The third pitch, Point Five Gully. *A. Kimber*

E/23   Fourth pitch, Point Five Gully. *A. Kimber*

E/24   Above major difficulties, Point Five Gully. *A. Kimber*

E/25   Looking across to Carn Dearg with North East Buttress left (fp = first platform) and beyond Tower Ridge. DB = Douglas Boulder, a = access chimney, Et = Eastern Traverse on the Tower, Gt = Great Tower, NC = North Castle Gully. *H. MacInnes*

E/26   Crux pitch, Vanishing Gully. *A. Kimber*

E/27   Gardyloo Buttress, first pitch, Smith's Route. *A. Kimber*

E/28   Near top of Italian Climb. *P. Moores*

E/29   West Face, Tower Ridge, looking over Garadh na Ciste. CA = Carn Mor Dearg Arête, PB = Pinnacle Buttress, GT = Great Tower. Circles denote climbers, the right one is crossing Tower Gap. *H. MacInnes*

E/30   The Battlements, a short route on the Gully Two side of Tower Ridge final slopes. It is approached by a traverse on the summit side of Gully Two Buttress, grade III/IV. *H. MacInnes*

E/31   Gully Two, with Comb Gully on right. *H. MacInnes*

E/32   Comb Gully. *P. Moores*

E/33   Green Gully. *H. MacInnes*

E/34   Number Three Gully, climbers about to descend. This gully and Gully Four are good descent routes. *H. MacInnes*

E/35   Tower Ridge, Coire na Ciste and Carn Dearg. a = Route onto Douglas Boulder (DB) for Tower Ridge.

Between Gullies 3 and 4 is Creag Coire na Ciste with its gullies South, Centre and North. GT = Great Tower; SC and NC = South Castle and North Castle gullies. *H. MacInnes*

E/36 The Curtain, Carn Dearg. *M. Ross*

E/37 The Curtain, Carn Dearg. *A. Kimber*

E/38 A climber can be seen in profile on start of Route II Direct. *A. Kimber*

E/39 The Shadow, Carn Dearg. *P. Braithwaite*

E/40 The Shadow, Carn Dearg. *P. Braithwaite*

E/41 On a steep section of The Shadow. *P. Braithwaite*

E/42 Castle Corrie, Carn Dearg, showing normal approach route. From CIC Hut this is gained via small gully which leads through the rocks just under Gully 5. Make a rising TR to foot of Great Buttress. 7 = Raeburn's Buttress. *H. MacInnes.*

E/43 Waterfall Gully, Left Route. *A. Kimber*

E/44 Waterfall Gully. *A. Kimber*

E/45 Waterfall Gully, alternative start. *A. Kimber*

E/46 The cliffs of Coire Ardair, Creagh Meaghaidh from the lochside. Bellevue Buttress is to the left of Raeburn's Gully and Pinnacle Buttress is between Raeburn's Gully and Easy Gully. The Inner Coire is to the right. 7 = South Pipe. *H. MacInnes*

E/47 Creagh Meaghaidh, Inner Coire. Easy Gully (EG) on left. The Window is to right of face. 8, 8a = Staghorn and Staghorn Direct. *H. MacInnes*

E/48 Ritchie's Gully Direct. *G. Hunter*

E/49 Smith's Gully. *A. Riley*

E/50 South Post, Direct start. *J. Cleare*

E/51 Centre Post, Direct route above. *P. Moores*

E/52 Creagh Meaghaidh. Looking up Staghorn Direct (8a) with South Pipe (7P) and Staghorn (8) Gully above. C indicates climbers on Trespasser Buttress (T). *H. MacInnes*

E/53 Creagh Meaghaidh, the crux of Trespasser Buttress (upper buttress). *H. MacInnes*

E/54 Pumpkin. *J. Cleare*

E/55 The Wand. *G. Hunter*

E/56 Diadem start. *P. Moores*

E/57 Buachaille Etive Mor as seen from the Glencoe road. J = access from car park at 'Jacksonville'. L = access from Lagangarbh. 3 = Curved Ridge. GG = Great Gully. N = North Buttress. Cg = Crowberry Gully. CR = Crowberry Ridge. 2 = D Gully Buttress. Normal route down is behind right hand skyline to top of Coire Tulaich and then down to Lagangarbh and Altnafeidh. *H. MacInnes*

E/58 Crowberry Gully and Crowberry Ridge. CT = Crowberry Tower. *H. MacInnes*

E/59 Great Gully and Raven's Gully. The edge of North Buttress is on the left. *H. MacInnes*

E/60 Curved Ridge and the Rannoch Wall. Curved Ridge is 3, Agag's Groove is 5 and Route 1 is 6. *H. MacInnes*

E/61 The Buachaille from the Glen Etive road. C = Chasm. LG = Ladies' Gully. *H. MacInnes*

E/62 The Chasm of Buachaille Etive Mor with a big build-up of snow. It is seldom in such easy conditions. *H. MacInnes*

E/63 Crowberry Tower and the normal route to the summit of the Buachaille from the top of Curved Ridge. At the Gap (top of Crowberry Gully Left Fork) the route to summit goes up left, by chimney/gully. A route up this front edge of the Tower is grade II/III, descent to Gap. *H. MacInnes*

E/64 Pitch two, Route 1, Rannoch Wall, Curved Ridge below. *H. MacInnes*

E/65 At the junction with the Direct Finish, Raven's Gully, Buachaille Etive Mor. *P. Moores*

E/66 Dalness Chasm, L = Left Fork, C = Central, R = Right. J = junction. From the Glen Etive road. *H. MacInnes*

E/67 Above the junction in the right fork of Dalness Chasm. *H. MacInnes*

E/68   Beinn Ceitlein, Glen Etive, DC = Deirdre's Cleft, as
        seen from the Glen Etive road just east of Dalness
        House. *H. MacInnes*
E/69   The start of Deirdre's Cleft. *C. Williamson*
E/70   Looking down to the Glen Etive road from Deirdre's
        Cleft. *H. MacInnes*
E/71   Sron na Lairig, Glencoe. Access via the Lairig Eilde,
        between Beinn Fhada and Buachaille Etive Beag.
        Gully 1 is grade III and Gully 3 an easy gully to top.
        H. MacInnes
E/72   On Sron na Lairig. *H. MacInnes*
E/73   A view of the Three Sisters from near the Meeting of
        the Waters. 4 = access route for Beinn Fhada, which
        skirts across hillside from bridge, then up obvious
        gully. LV = Lost Valley. 1 = Route to Bealach Dearg.
        LVB = Lost Valley Buttress. ZZ = Zigzags (access to
        Stob Coire nan Lochan). 3 = Alternative route into
        Coire nan Lochan valley, but not as good as 5. B =
        bridges. R = Start for Aonach Eagach Ridge.
        H. MacInnes
E/74   The ridge of Gearr Aonach with Stob Coire na
        Lochan behind. Below left is the Lost Valley.
        H. MacInnes
E/75   Looking over the Lost Valley (lower part, LV), with
        Gearr Aonach and the Aonach Eagach Ridge
        behind. The main road is out of sight between these
        two ridges. E = easy descent line off Aonach
        Eagach to main road and also the route up to ridge
        (alternatively take the valley on right, Coire Ruigh).
        Z = Zigzag, 1 = Farm Gully, 2 = Twenty Minute
        Gully, 3 = The Chancellor. *H. MacInnes*
E/76   The chockstone, Peregrine Gully, Lost Valley below.
        H. MacInnes
E/77   Rev. Ted's Gully, Centre Branch, Lost Valley.
        H. MacInnes
E/78   The head of the Lost Valley with the route to
        Bealach Dearg (BD). BL = Bealach.

1. Descent route from head of Lost Valley, sometimes small cornice.

2. Descent route from Bidean/Stob Coire nan Lochan Bealach. Keep to line indicated on descent as waterfall pitch, visible just above junction of routes, is dangerous.

3. Easy face route up Stob Coire Sgreamhach (A), 3497ft.

4. Access route to col at bottom section of Stob Coire Sgreamhach summit ridge.

5, 7, 9, 10, 14, 15, 16. All winter gully climbs of up to Grade II standard.

6. Chimney Route, 240ft, Grade IV. This climb follows a very prominent chimney splitting corrie face of buttress and gives a series of problems over icy chockstones.

8. Granny's Groove, Grade III. This is the R branch of 7. Go up steep scoop sometimes with overhang, turned on L.

12. Right-Hand Gully, 200ft, Grade II. A pleasant gully climb sometimes giving an ice pitch above a cave. Usually cornice at top.

13. Short Gully, 100ft, Grade II. The narrow chimney/gully to R of easy snow couloir. Sometimes an ice pitch at top. C = Summit of Stob Coire nan Lochan. NEr = NE ridge. *H. MacInnes*

331

above steep section of gully. *H. MacInnes*

E/84 The West Face of Beinn Fhada from the Lost Valley. B = Gully climb of Grade I. Best approach to this buttress is up from left end of Lost Valley floor (flat area) and then directly up to lower rock buttress on left of photograph. Best access to main buttress on right is by true left of gully G from true right path up Lost Valley. *H. MacInnes*

E/85 The upper East face, Gearr Aonach showing Gully A = (A) and Lost Leeper = (LL). The path passes beneath this face after rising from floor of Lost Valley. 10, 11, 12 = Rev. Ted's Route. *H. MacInnes*

E/86 The west face of Gearr Aonach from the summit of Aonach Dubh. Beyond are the gullies on the west face of Beinn Fhada, across the Lost Valley. 6 = The Wasp. 7 = The Cleg. 8 = Main Buttress. 9 = Twine Climb. 10 = The Ramp. The Stob Coire nan Lochan path goes up the valley in the foreground on the true right of the stream. *H. MacInnes*

E/87 The exit of the through route 999, West Face, Gearr Aonach. *H. MacInnes*

E/88 Stob Coire nan Lochan from the Gearr Aonach Ridge. On the left above climber is the exit of McArtney's Gully. a and c = access routes. b = easy route to summit via ridge (also a descent route from West Face of Aonach Dubh). 2 = Boomerang Gully, Left Branch. *H. MacInnes*

E/89 Stob Coire nan Lochan. *H. MacInnes*

E/90 The cornice, North Gully, Stob Coire nan Lochan. *H. MacInnes*

E/91 Evening Citizen, Stob Coire nan Lochan. *H. MacInnes*

E/92 Dorsal Arête, Stob Coire nan Lochan. *H. MacInnes*

E/93 The north face of Aonach Dubh. O = Ossian's Cave. p = Pleasant Terrace. DG = Deep Gash Gully. *H. MacInnes*

E/94 The Cave Pitch, Ossian's Close, Aonach Dubh North Face. *H. MacInnes*

E/95 Findlay's Rise, North Face, Aonach Dubh.
H. MacInnes

E/96 Findlay's Rise, North Face, Aonach Dubh. *N. Keir*

E/97 Bidean nam Bian. BL = Bealach. L = Left branch
Central Gully, Grade II. CP = Collie's Pinnacle.
Diamond Buttress left; Churchdoor right.
H. MacInnes

E/98 On the left S = the route down from Stob Coire nan
Lochan to the bealach between the upper Lost Valley
and the Bidean Coire. 2 = descent route from
Bidean/Stob Coire nan Lochan Bealach. The route
marked 4 should only be descended by competent
parties. B = the route to Bidean. D = Diamond
Buttress. CP = Collie's Pinnacle. Ct = Crypt route.
C = top of this route, shared with West Chimney.
E = easy route onto Bidean–Stob Coire nam Beith
ridge. *H. MacInnes*

E/99 Looking towards the summit of Bidean nam Bian
from the ridge leading to Stob Coire nam Beith. CDB
= Church Door Buttress. A climber can be seen in
Hourglass Gully (A). *H. MacInnes*

E/100 The three exit routes from Central Gully, Bidean
nam Bian. No. 1 is the hardest, Grade II.
H. MacInnes

E/101 The step across the gap on Church Door Buttress,
Bidean nam Bian: Crypt and West Chimney routes.
H. MacInnes

E/102 The steep chimney above climber, Church Door
Buttress, West Chimney and Crypt routes.
H. MacInnes

E/103 Stob Coire nam Beith = B. E to F = easy route from
Glencoe. Circles denote climbers. BL = Bealach
between upper Lost Valley and Bidean Coire. D =
Diamond Buttress. C = Church Door Buttress. S =
Summit Gully. L. = Adagio. *H. MacInnes*

E/104 Stob Coire nam Beith. R = ascent/descent route
from col. *H. MacInnes*

E/105 Stob Coire nam Beith, NW Face. D = easy route to col. S = Summit Gully. *H. MacInnes*

E/106 Adagio, Stob Coire nam Beith. *H. MacInnes*

E/107 The West Face of Aonach Dubh. d = Dinnertime Buttress. i = the icicle, Elliot's Downfall. B to G = buttresses. Cy to V = The Rake. *H. MacInnes*

E/108 The Screen. *E. Grindlay*

E/109 A telephoto of Gully 4. Top circle denotes climbers at top of E Buttress. CC = Christmas Couloir. CE = Christmas Eaves. *H. MacInnes*

E/110 The Slot, West Face, Aonach Dubh. *H. MacInnes*

E/111 Elliot's Downfall (the icicle), West Face, Aonach Dubh. *J. Leinster*

E/112 Gully 6, West Face, Aonach Dubh. *M. Ross*

E/113 Clachaig Gully, Glencoe. A descent route follows the true right bank. *H. MacInnes*

E/114 Creag Bhan, Glean-leac-na-muidhe. A telephoto taken from just west of Information Centre. Mc Dr = MacDonald's Direct, a Grade I climb. *H. MacInnes*

E/115 Sgor na h'Ulaidh. A view from the approach via Gleann-leac-na-muidhe. R = descent route. *H. MacInnes*

E/116 The start of the Beinn a' Bheithir ridge as seen from Ballachulish. The route (a) starts just beyond Gorteneorn farm (west side of river Laroch). An alternative route to the summit is also marked. *H. MacInnes*

E/117 A telephoto of the access ridge to the first summit, Sgorr Bhan. Grade I-II. *H. MacInnes*

E/118 On the Beinn a' Bheithir ridge. Descent can be down the corrie leading NE into Gleann a' Chaolais, beyond Sgorr Dhonuill. This leads down to the A828 at the Ballachulish Narrows. *H. MacInnes*

E/119 Garbh Bheinn, Ardgour, as seen from across Loch Linnhe. GR = Great Ridge, a Grade III climb. Access via Corran Ferry and Coir' an Iubhair, seldom in suitable winter conditions. *H. MacInnes*

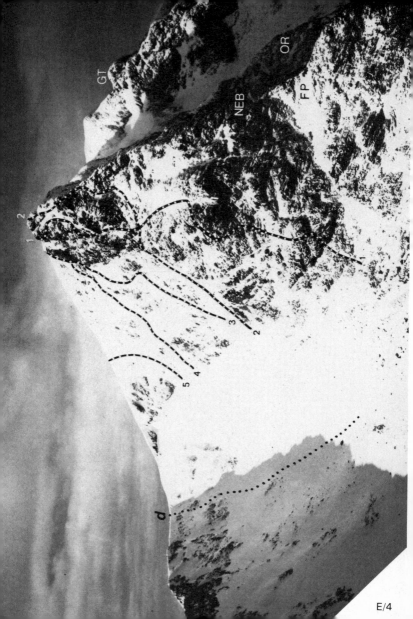

GT OR NEB FP 1 2 2 3 4 5 d

E/4

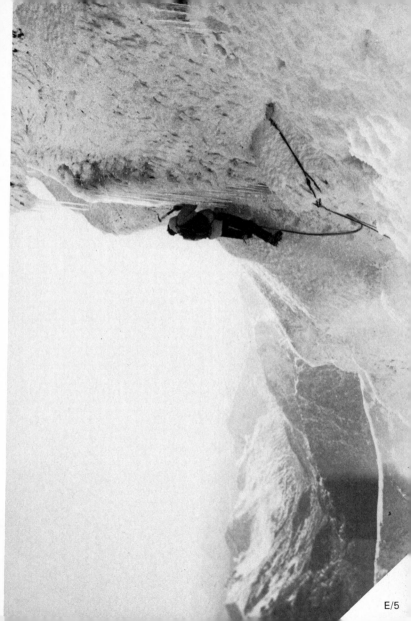

E/5

NEB
Od SL
Or
Ob
F
Gg
CA
.5
fP
z
-1
-2
S -3

E/6

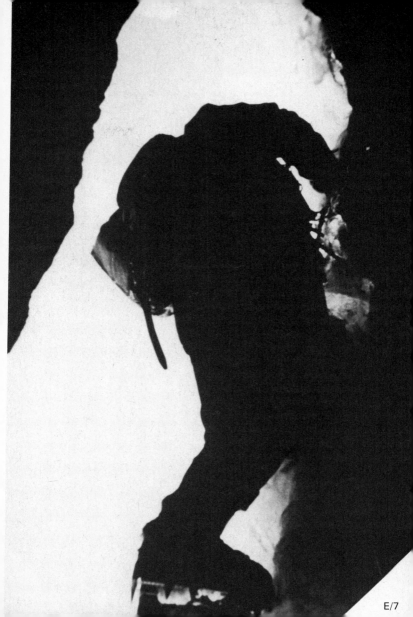

E/7

E/8

E/9

E/10

E/11

C

E/12

Et

E/15

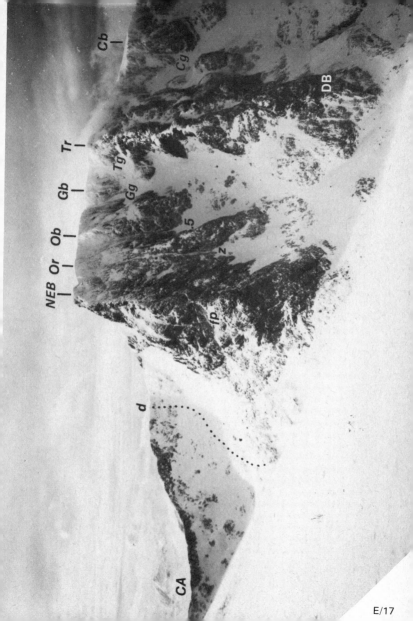

E/18

E/20

E/21

E/22

E/23

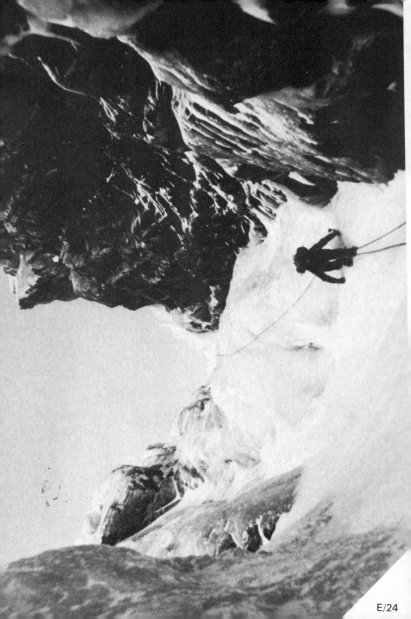

E/24

E/25

E/26

E/28

E/29

E/32

E/34

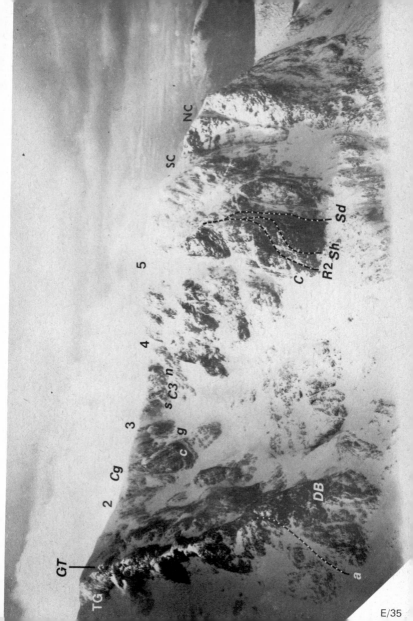

E/35

E/36

E/37

E/38

E/39

E/42

E/43

E/44

E/45

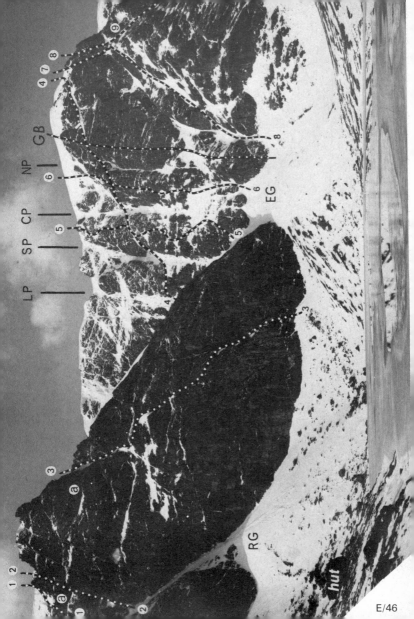

E/46

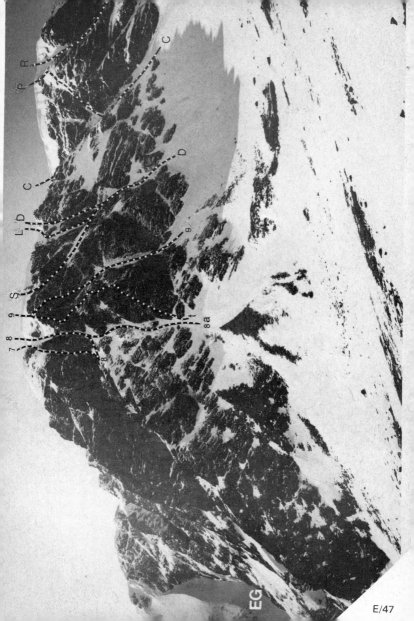

E/49

E/54

E/55

E/56

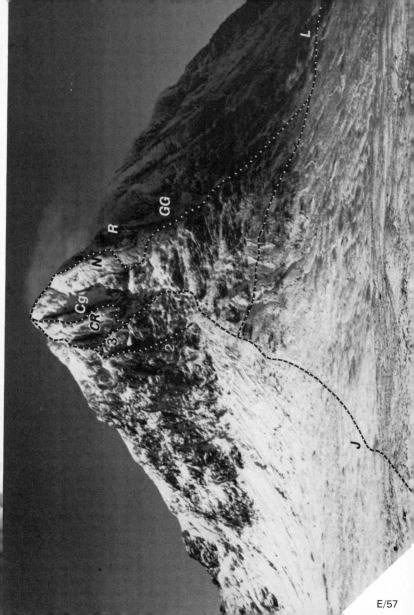

E/57

E/59

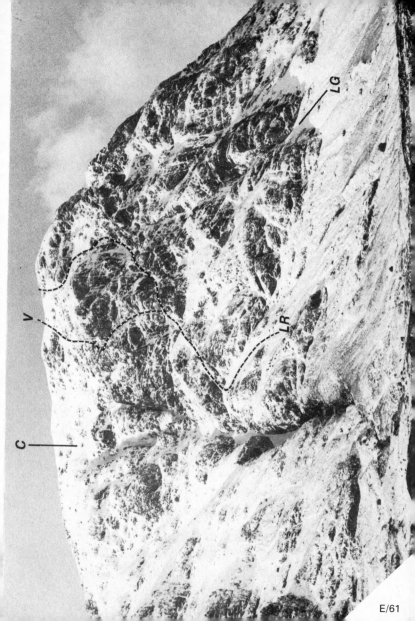

E/61

E/62

E/63

E/64

E/65

E/67

DC

E/68

E/70

E/72

E/73

E/74

E/75

E/76

C

14

NEr

Bidean Nam Bian

BL

Lost Valley

13

16 12

9 10

7 8

5 6

15

2

4

1

3

BD

A

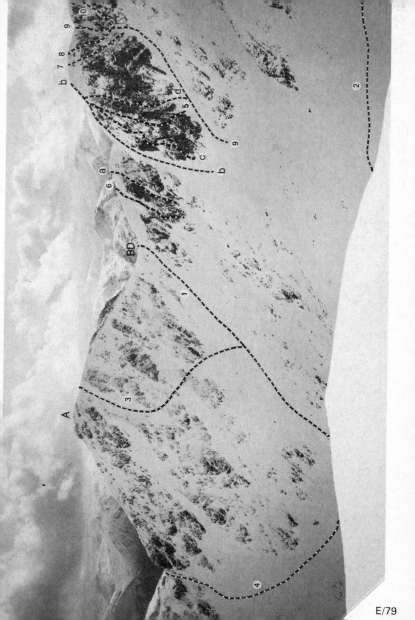

E/79

E/80

E/81

E/82

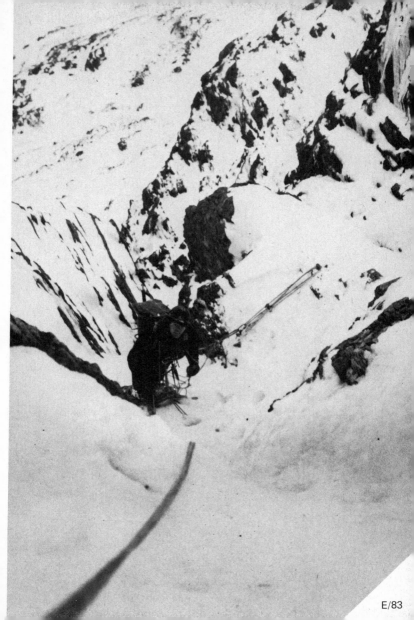

E/83

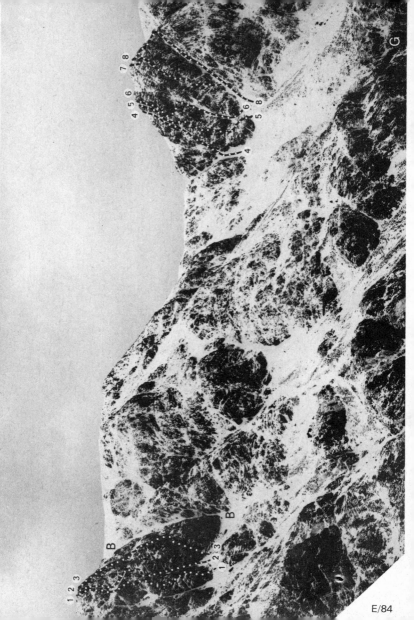

E/84

E/85

E/86

E/88

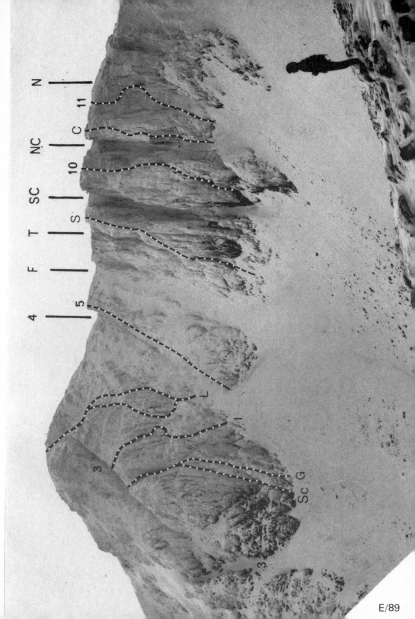

E/89

E/90

E/92

E/94

E/96

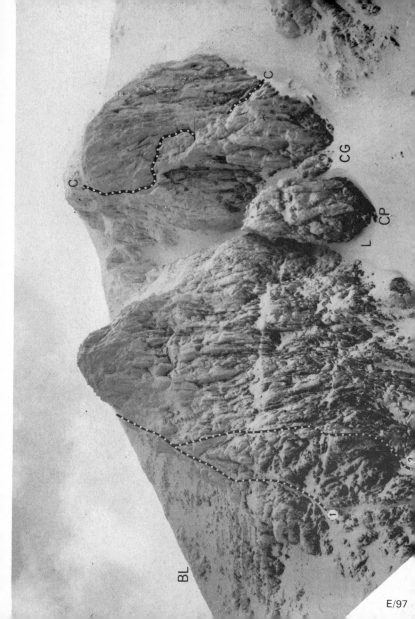

BL

C

C

CG

CP

L

1

2

E/97

E/98

Bidean

CDB

E/101

E/102

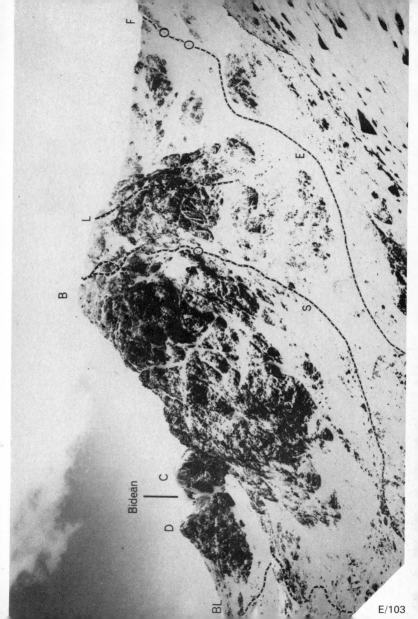

E/103

E/104

E/105

E/106

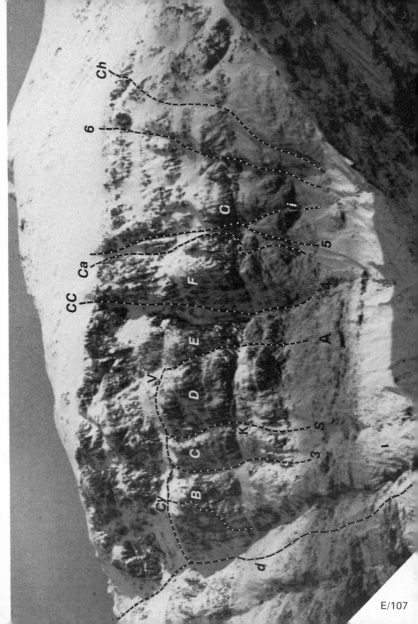

E/107

E/108

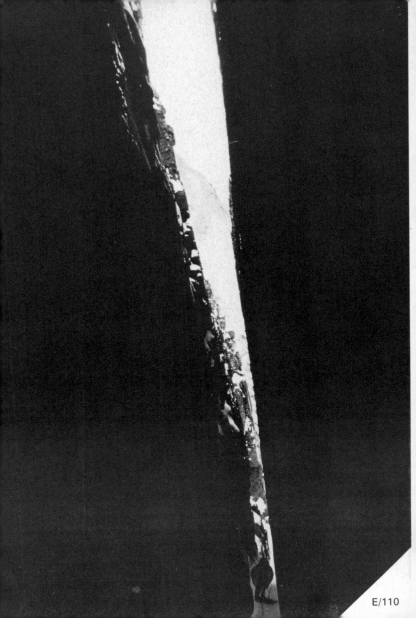

E/110

E/111

E/112

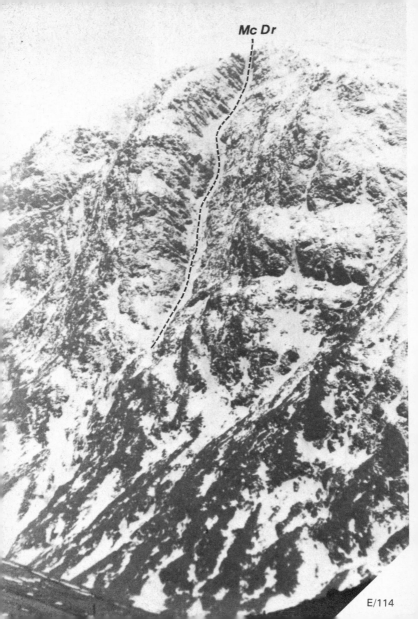

Mc Dr

E/115

E/117

E/118

GR

E/119

E/121

E/122

Am Bodach

om

bc

d

v

3

2

1

E/123

Am Bodach

d

2

BC

om

3

V

1

E/124

E/125

E/126

E/127

CC

E/128

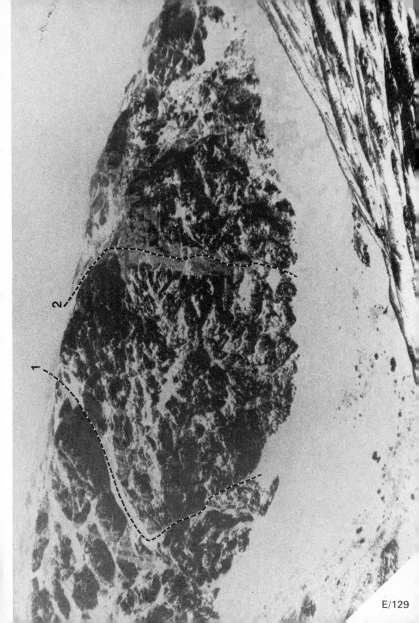

E/130

AREA F

The Cobbler
Map: OS No. 56, Loch Lomond, 1:50,000

This mini-peak stands in jagged isolation above Loch Long and is seen to advantage from the village of Arrochar. It is not really a winter mountain, but when conditions are favourable it can offer short but fine winter lines. The usual approach is from the A83 at the Torpedo Testing Station near the head of Loch Long and thence by the Buttermilk Burn path. Alternatively, leave from Succoth Farm and take the slanting path up past the Narnain Boulder to reach the corrie.

Access Route (1)
An easy snow slope leading to Centre Peak.

Centre Gully (2) grade II 400ft
This is a straightforward gully climb which sometimes has an awkward cornice to overcome.

Ramshead Gully (R) grade III 300ft
Climb easily to iced chockstone (crux). Gully widens above. Exit R at top after steep pitch.

Recess Route (3) grade III/IV 250ft
Ascend wall to ledges, 50ft. TR R to niche below bulge, climb to top of block; 25ft. Up diagonal chimney to snowy ledge below nail-marked (or iced) chimney, 15ft. Climb direct to overhang, pass with R TR finishing at deep recess, 40ft. Ascend deep smooth-walled chimney, exit on L, 25ft. Easy up ledges to terrace. (NB: Possible to escape down Ramshead Gully at this point.) Go 30ft R into groove (the Fold). Climb this on L. Above ascend cave on L to gain easy snow to top.

Great Gully (4) grade II 200ft
A straightforward gully sometimes holding some ice.

The Cobbler. A view from above Arrochar showing, left to right; the South Peak, which can make an interesting winter traverse, the Centre Peak (summit) and the North Peak.
H. MacInnes

Bibliography

Blackshaw, Alan, *Mountaineering, from Hill Walking to Alpine Climbing*, Penguin 1970

Chouinard, Yvon, *Climbing Ice*, Sierra Club Books 1978

Fraser, Colin, *Avalanches and Snow Safety*, John Murray (first published as *Avalanche Enigma* 1966)

Murray, W.H., *Mountaineering in Scotland*, J.M. Dent 1947

March, W., *Modern Rope Management Techniques in Mountaineering*, Cicerone Press 1972

Mountain Rescue and Cave Rescue, Mountain Rescue Committee

Patey, Tom, *One Man's Mountains*, Gollancz 1971

Index

476

480